DATE DUE

DEMCO 38-297

ASK *the* DOCTORS

ASK *the* DOCTORS

*Questions and Answers from
"The Minirth-Meier Clinic" Broadcast*

FRANK B. MINIRTH
& PAUL D. MEIER
w i t h KEVIN KINBACK

BAKER BOOK HOUSE
Grand Rapids, Michigan

Printed in the United States of America

Library of Congress Cataloging-in-Publication Data

Minirth, Frank B.
    Ask the doctors : questions and answers from "The Minirth-Meier
Clinic" broadcast / Frank B. Minirth and Paul D. Meier with Kevin
Kinback.
    p.   cm.
    ISBN: 0-8010-6280-2
    1. Mental health—Religious aspects—Christianity—Miscellanea.
2. Christian life—Miscellanea.   I. Meier, Paul D.   II. Kinback, Kevin.
III. Title.
BT732.4.M54   1991
261.5'15—dc20   91-6905
                                                        CIP

Contents

Preface

Christians today want to know how to live happy, meaningful, and practical Christian lives in spite of the trials and difficulties they may be facing. They want to know how to survive the grief and losses that seem to be a necessary part of life.

As psychiatrists with seminary training, Drs. Minirth and Meier have been discussing life's tough questions with millions of listeners on their live national radio broadcast, "The Minirth-Meier Clinic." Annually the doctors treat thousands of patients at several Minirth-Meier clinics located throughout the United States.

With the help of Kevin Kinback, a dedicated medical student and friend of Drs. Minirth and Meier, the material presented in this book is gleaned from questions and answers heard on their radio broadcast. They reflect the questions most often asked by concerned listeners and in fact mirror issues faced by thoughtful Christians today. Often Drs. Minirth and Meier added to the material given in their radio answers to allow a fuller explanation in this book.

The answers given are intended to provide initial help or understanding. If you desire a more thorough discussion of a problem, write to the Minirth-Meier Clinic, Box 1925, Richardson, Texas 75085, for a list of additional publications which address specific topics. Call 1-800-545-1819 for information about the Minirth-Meier Clinic nearest you.

We wish to express sincere gratitude to Kevin Kinback. In spite of the immense pressures of being a medical student, Kevin listened to the hundreds of hours of radio broadcasts of "The Minirth-Meier Clinic" to glean and summarize the most frequently asked questions.

We also appreciate the patience and perseverance of the Baker Book House editorial team which put the manuscript into book form.

1

A Christian's Approach to Mental and Emotional Health

In today's tension-filled, rapidly changing world, many people have a fascination with current psychological theory, especially if they are shown how to apply its principles and techniques to their own coping mechanisms. The shelves in public libraries, bookstores, and even some private homes display an intriguing collection of brightly jacketed publications, all claiming to divulge the secrets of achieving sound, "mentally healthy" lifestyles.

Most of these self-help manuals address the negative end of the mental-health continuum by bombarding the reader with advice about such varied problems as "emotional dysfunctioning," "alienation," "borderline personality," and a host of other frightening catchwords. Few attempt to frame a workable set of criteria for determining just *who* is "mentally healthy" and who is not, mainly because the degree of one's so-called emotional stability cannot be accurately measured by any objective test or device yet known. Of course, even a layperson can tell when someone is mentally "ill" to the point of needing professional care—for example, when there are symptoms of suicidal intention, uncontrollable violence, hallucinatory or delusional experiences, or emotional distress that has caused total motivational paralysis or insomnia or life-threatening eating disorders. Other signs of emotional pain are more subtle and thus harder to spot. It is principally these gray areas that we address in this book, which is essentially a set of questions and answers that is representative of those concerns we see daily in our counseling practice. Some of these problems require professional help; others respond fairly well to attempts at self-healing.

The Body-Mind-Soul Connection

Anyone who is "healthy" (in the broad sense of the word) is free of disease, pain, and malfunctioning on all *three* levels of his or her personhood—sound in "body, mind, and soul," so to speak. We believe, as do many other professional health-providers, that these three separate dimensions of human nature interact so closely that "health" on one level always impinges on "health" on the other two in one way or another. For example, the state of our mental/emotional health affects our physical well-being, and vice versa. The clichéed "mind over matter" idea has proven to have considerable validity. Physicians daily confirm that patients with strong coping techniques (a "healthy attitude") can minimize the effects or course of a disease process, or at the very least make the symptoms and pain easier to bear. This further verifies the long-standing belief that a physical disorder—such as asthma or ulcers—can have an emotional component. Some rather recent research and related case histories suggest that certain organic diseases—including cancer—*may* be influenced through the focusing of one's mental energies on the recovery process. This, of course, should come as no great surprise to the millions of Christian believers who have confidence in the *power* of prayer.

To take the body-mind-soul connection one step further, we believe that spiritual health—the depth of our relationship to God and the extent to which we follow his biblically inscribed guidelines—affects our ability to handle both our physical afflictions and our mental/emotional distress. Therefore, our professional counseling is "Christian." This means that in addition to using scientifically based principles, we offer spiritual suggestions that are appropriate to the situation and mindset of the counselees—whether their problem is loneliness, depression, emotional baggage from the past, uncontrolled violence, marital conflict, or any other "mental health" concern.

Biblical Guidelines for Mental Health

It is our firm belief that the search for wisdom in the Scriptures is foundational to spiritual maturity, which in turn both eases our adjustment to the demands of daily living and enhances our ability to form meaningful human relationships. Of course, personal acceptance of Jesus Christ as Savior and Lord is the basis for any Christian's faith life, but that alone is not quite enough to satisfy all our human longing or even to fulfill God's blueprint for an individual's life.

Instead, there is no better summary of what is expected of a child of God than Matthew 22:37–39. When Jesus was asked by an expert in Mosaic Law to describe God's most important requirement, he replied:

"Love the Lord your God with all your heart and with all your soul and with all your mind." This is the first and greatest commandment. And the second is like it: "Love your neighbor as yourself." All the Law and the Prophets hang on these two commandments.

These simple words also spell out the three essential elements for sound mental health: (1) intimacy with God; (2) love for one's fellowman; and (3) proper self-love. The latter is perhaps the hardest for most people to understand, much less accept. Yet the failure to do so can be the cause of considerable emotional distress. "Proper self-love" is based first on the fact that we were created "in God's image"—although in Eden the divine plan for perfect man's dominion over a perfect world was perverted by human sinfulness. However, because God loved us enough to offer his Son as redemption for our failures, we were saved by his blood and can be reborn as "worthy" individuals once again.

Listed below are some biblical guidelines that will facilitate anyone's struggle for "happy," practical Christian living. *Balance*, after all, is what good health is really about. Consider these suggestions as a set of exercises to build up your mental strength, improve your emotional muscle tone, and sharpen your moral perceptions. You will notice that the guidelines reflect the three major areas of concern singled out in God's "greatest commandment." They should prove helpful, even if you also decide to seek guidance for your problems with a trained counselor.

Love the Lord your God

1. *Daily commit your life to the purpose of glorifying God.* Start each morning by thanking God for another chance to enjoy the world he created. This will help you see each new day as a fresh opportunity to please God and become more Christlike. Ask God in prayer for strength to face whatever temptations and challenges will be placed before you that day.

2. *Spend regular times in prayerful meditation on God's eternal truths as found in Holy Scripture.* To discover the interconnection between your spiritual fullness and mental health, you must program your brain's "computer chips" to think God's way—unselfishly. Left to

implement our own self-serving schemes, we cannot count on achieving long-term "success" or contentment.

3. *Learn to enjoy reading the Word of God by setting aside a regular daily time for Bible study.* The more you become familiar with its teachings, the more you will recognize how the Bible applies to your daily walk. Nothing else can do more to strengthen you in times of trouble. The apostle Paul said, "Now I commit you to God and to the word of his grace, which can build you up and give you an inheritance among all those who are sanctified" (Acts 20:32). Let the Word of God govern your life. It will correct you, but it will also nurture your faith lovingly.

4. *Accept God as your primary support system.* If you have accepted Christ as Lord and Savior, you belong to God and in him you have a support system that never fails. Although troubles come, Christ will sustain you. He has promised that "everyone who hears these words of mine and puts them into practice is like a wise man who built his house on the rock. The rain came down, the streams rose, and the winds blew and beat against that house; yet it did not fall, because it had its foundation on the rock" (Matt. 7:24–25). With God as our main root of support, we will stand firm when the gusts of personal tribulation blow in our direction. We can be "like a tree planted by streams of water, which yields its fruit in season and whose leaf does not wither" (Ps. 1:3) Let God teach you how to bend with circumstances beyond your control—to accept and adapt to adversity.

5. *Avoid sin and temptation.* Nothing destroys mental acuity and emotional peace more surely than a guilty conscience. The apostle Paul warned against "whatever belongs to [our] earthly nature: sexual immorality, impurity, lust, evil desires and greed, which is idolatry" (Col. 3:5). Our best defense against the devil's schemes is to put on "the full armor of God" and take a firm stand against evil (cf. Eph. 6:10–13).

Love your neighbor

6. *Cherish your family ties.* Your spouse, children, parents, and siblings are meant to comprise your strongest support system. Remember to acknowledge that support by frequent applications of love and affirmation within your family circle. Resist the temptation to "avenge" wrongs committed by family members. Instead, concentrate on being a peacemaker, leaving the rest to God.

7. *Spend time each week in fellowship with committed Christian friends.* John Donne's seventeenth-century words still ring true today: "No man is an island, entire of itself. . . . I am involved in mankind; and therefore never send to know for whom the bell tolls; it tolls for thee." Close friends are no luxury; they are *necessary* for long-term mental health. Of course, friendships do require effort and discriminating taste. Select your friends very carefully; you will become more and more like them: "He who walks with the wise grows wise, but a companion of fools suffers harm" (Prov. 13:20). Spend time with your friends. Share their joys and their sorrows. (Although it is not necessary to shy away completely from non-Christian friendships, the greatest degree of intimacy will be found among others who share your commitment to God and his Son.)

8. *Rid yourself of the roots of bitterness.* Grudges over real or imagined wrongs will fester and lie deeply buried in your consciousness. Determine not to let unresolved anger rob you of peace and joy. Always remember to examine your own responsibility in a conflict: "Each one should test his own actions. Then he can take pride in himself, without comparing himself to somebody else" (Gal. 6:4). We are to "bear with each other," forgiving grievances as the Lord forgave us (Col. 3:13). Most importantly, we are to rid ourselves of "bitterness, rage and anger" and be kind and compassionate to one another (Eph. 6:32–33).

9. *Concentrate on reaching out to one needy person*

each week. It is through servanthood that we bring Christ's love to others. Help with a chore, visit a shut-in, deliver a "friendship gift," share a burden, offer counsel, have devotions with someone you know. Getting more involved in the lives of other people in your community will help keep your mind off your own problems—which may pale in comparison to what others are facing.

10. *Develop dependability.* Work on being someone who can be counted on to be loving, gentle, forgiving, and understanding in a crisis. You will earn the respect of others, which—as an added bonus—will make you feel good about yourself.

Love yourself

11. *Work on building a realistic self-concept.* See yourself as a child of God who has been given special gifts and abilities. Evaluate those talents and determine to use them in the Lord's service as you accept the fact that you are a worthwhile person for whom Christ died.

12. *Develop an unwavering purpose in life.* If you devote your life to Christ and his goals, you can build on this foundation and pursue lasting achievement. Leaving a legacy of love should be one of your primary motivators.

13. *Strive for excellence in your career.* Here is a special opportunity to develop feelings of competence. Set a realistic long-term goal for your professional life, but one that is reachable in progressively higher steps. If you cannot *possibly* reach an objective, you are setting up a self-fulfilling prophecy of "failure." Concentrate on dreams that are achievable with diligent effort. Remember that the career of "housewife" and "mother" are as high a calling in God's perspective as being a world leader. Don't be swayed by worldly prejudices.

14. *Work on leading a balanced life.* Have a daily routine that brings you personal satisfaction, including career, recreation, family sharing, household projects, ministry to others, and so on. Work and play with enthusiasm, but avoid extremes. Take time out to pray and to

think, but also to feel. Be serious about the important things, but develop a healthy sense of humor that can help you chuckle at life's struggles before your soul has time to dive into depression. It is not a sin to enjoy yourself—and laughter can relieve as much tension as a torrent of tears. Plan some time each day when you are finished with your list of things to do and simply relax with nothing scheduled.

15. *Whenever possible, avoid placing yourself in stressful situations.* Although mature Christians can withstand the tension of changing conditions and conflict better than most people, everyone has a breaking point. Learn to recognize your limitations and don't tempt destiny by pushing yourself too hard.

16. *Seek help if you need it.* Don't let false pride stand in the way of getting the advice and counsel you may need, whether for a sudden "emergency" or long-term distress. God tells us often to seek a multitude of counselors. He wants you to be happy!

2

Freedom from
Emotional Bondage

God gave human beings the wonderful gift of emotional expression to broaden our experiencing of the universe far beyond what our five senses perceive and our intellectual abilities process in our brain cells. Because we have "feelings," we can appreciate the miracles of nature and the beauty of manmade artistry and are able to enjoy rich relationships with our fellow humans. Emotions color our world. Our basic survival needs focus on self-preservation, but even the "negative" emotions—anger, fear, grief—not only protect us from potential harm but, when properly channeled, can also motivate us toward greater Christlikeness. Too often we deny our emotions or hide from them; we even devise complicated defense mechanisms to disguise the way we really feel. Recognizing our feelings and understanding why they exist are the first steps in learning how to liberate ourselves from their control and then use them to add joy, fulfillment, and affirmation to our own lives and those of others.

What follows is a discussion of the most common questions our staff hears about emotions. Read with the intent of loosening the restraints you may have placed on your feelings and determining to take charge of any emotions that have imprisoned you in their power.

What are the main types and causes of emotional pain? I hear a lot about people who "suffer emotionally," but I'm not sure I know what that means.

There are three primary sources of emotional pain:

Lack of self worth—a low self-concept. This may seem obvious, but how can it happen? The answer often lies in a lack of affirmation from "significant others"—mainly parents—during the formative years of early childhood. For example, parents may place exaggerated and unrealistic demands on their first child. Simply because of this pressure, the oldest child in a family tends to be the most "successful" in terms of a career. Unfortunately, happiness is not so easily obtained, since these children seldom believe they have achieved enough to please their demanding parents. Such parents often suffer great emotional pain from their own low self-esteem, triggered by a faulty value system which says money, prestige, power, control, or sexual prowess give meaning to life. Our true worth is based on our position in Christ and our personal walk with him.

Firstborn offspring often comment that their parents seemed only halfway satisfied with their efforts during childhood, always urging them to try harder and do even better, to "set a good example." They carry this obsession with achievement into adulthood. Then, grappling with the new challenge of self-appraisal, they can measure their worth only in terms of visible success and wonder why that is not enough to satisfy them.

The youngest child, on the other hand, is often smothered and overprotected. Hating to see her "baby" grow up and reluctant to let go, a mother may allow the youngest child—particularly a son—to become overly dependent on her. Because this son then feels he cannot be successful without her help, he nurses a low sense of self-worth. Or a doting father may wish to protect a daughter from the demands and dangers of a cruel world outside the security of the home and keep her his "little girl" forever. He, too, is sending a subtle message that she cannot survive on her own capacities.

The presence of a cold, preoccupied parent spells "rejection" and low self-esteem in any child. Having a passive or absent parent is equally unsettling. Also, if an infant receives too little physical and verbal attention beyond attention to his or her basic needs, this can trigger early development of problems with self-worth.

Childhood is generally the time of life when self-esteem must be properly established. Rarely does a well-adjusted child mature into adulthood and suddenly develop a poor self-image. Since the defeats of childhood are entrenched beneath the surface of our feelings and memories, overcoming them can be difficult. Simply remembering them is painful enough. Encourage your children to tell you about their painful experiences. Compliment them when you see them developing godly character traits.

Lack of intimacy with others—or loneliness. Humans are social beings; we are designed by God to need one another. This has been so since Adam, of whom God said, "It is not good that he is alone." But human beings are also basically selfish. We like having our own way, even at the expense of loved ones and friendships. This egocentrism often leads to superficiality in relationships, which in the long run produces loneliness.

Loneliness, like happiness, is a choice, although lonely people rarely realize that they are actually deciding to lead a solitary life. Many loners imagine that other people do not want to get close to them, when in reality they are rejecting any intimacy that may be offered. In their imaginations they blame others, choosing to ignore their own responsibility in the matter.

This defense mechanism, known as *projection*, superimposes one's own behavior and feelings onto others. Like a slide projector that throws a photographic image onto a screen, these individuals see in others their own unwillingness to yield some of their autonomy in favor of a give-and-take relationship. They have chosen to be lonely, yet hold others accountable for their pain.

An excellent description of projection and its hypocrisy is Jesus' teaching in Matthew 7:3–5:

> Why do you look at the speck of sawdust in your brother's eye and pay no attention to the plank in your own eye? How can you say to your brother, "Let me take the speck out of your eye," when all the time there is a plank in your own eye? You hypocrite, first take the plank out of your own eye, and then you will see clearly to remove the speck from your brother's eye.

Lack of intimacy with God. Deep within each human is a God-shaped vacuum—an inner emptiness that can be filled only by a personal relationship with God through Jesus Christ. Although in our professional practice we serve patients from every religious background imaginable, within two or three sessions nearly every troubled patient brings up some spiritual problem that is intensifying his or her emotional pain. At the heart of these problems is an awareness of sinfulness and a need for cleansing, which can be achieved only through God and his message of redemption.

How does emotional pain contribute to depression? Can God remove that pain?

Since all the above-mentioned sources of emotional pain, including poor self-esteem, involve the failure to achieve intimacy with others or with God, they can predispose a person toward accumulating grudges. This in turn may lead to "clinical depression," a long-term and overriding sense of hopeless despair.

Those who are suffering with emotional pain from a low self-concept often passively place the blame on others. They may be introverted, have few friends, and be prone to bouts of misery. The loneliness that follows closely on the heels of lacking intimate relationships is especially conducive to despair. Lonely people may either harbor grudges toward those who "reject" them or be angry with themselves for being (in their own eyes) so unacceptable. Medical science has proven that resentment—anger turned inward—contributes to the very real biochemical changes that characterize severe clinical depression.

What exactly are these physiological symptoms?

Patients usually first notice slowed body movements, a poor quality of sleep, and appetite changes—eating too much or too little. Some also experience gastrointestinal disturbances, irregular menstrual cycles, declined sexual interest, headaches, rapid heartbeat and heart palpitations, and hypochondriacal tendencies (having physical ailments seems preferable to acknowledging psychological conflicts).

Lacking true intimacy with God, yet desiring it, can also lead to depression, particularly if the person uses a standard defense mechanism of blaming God for everything that goes wrong. Generally, however, the intimacy has not developed because the person simply doesn't feel deserving of it.

Of course, none of us is worthy of a relationship with God. We are all sinners. Still, God loves us so much that he desires us to draw close to him anyway. That is why he paved the way for reestablishing intimacy through the death of his Son Jesus Christ. This was the payment for our sins—our unworthiness and imperfection as "fallen" humanity. A relationship with God is now dependent not on *our* merit but on *his* loving act of redemption—which bridges the chasm between us and makes us receptive to the divine power that can heal our emotional pain.

I worry a lot, and this causes me to be moody and even angry or irritable with others. What are some biblical ways to reduce my anxiety and fears?

First, it is important to understand that worry and the anger and frustration that often accompany it are normal human emotions. Scripture tells us in several passages not to succumb to worry (e.g., Matt. 6:25–34; Phil. 4:6–7). Naturally, the stronger our faith in God, the less we will worry, especially about problems that exist only in our minds. This doesn't mean we can simply attain perfect faith and escape the bonds of anxiety. That won't happen in this lifetime. Yet, if we strive to reach the goal of stronger faith, we can use our worry to motivate us to productive action rather than let it overcome us.

Where can you begin? Here are some ideas.

Organize your worries. When generalized anxiety crops up during the day, as it certainly will from time to time, don't allow yourself to surrender to its debilitating effect. Instead identify its source, write down the worry, and save it for a "worry time," maybe from nine to ten at night. During that time, concentrate on the specific worry (or worries) you have listed, pray about it, asking God what he would have you do about the situation.

Ask others' advice. Don't be too proud to go to friends for advice and counsel. The Bible says that friends can sharpen friends as iron sharpens iron (Prov. 27:17), and that "many advisors make victory sure" (Prov. 11:14; cf. 15:22 and 24:6). The advice of committed Christian companions may give you some valuable insight, since it comes from a more objective viewpoint than yours, which is colored by the burden of anxiety for the welfare of loved ones or yourself.

Consider the worst that can happen. Ask yourself, "What would happen if my worst worry came true?"

Then ask, "What would God teach me from that?" The majority of things we worry about never happen, and those that do usually are not as devastating as we expected them to be. Many things that seem bad at first later turn out to produce unimaginably good results. Afterward, when we look back and see how God was working even through our worries and misfortunes, we wonder why we worried in the first place.

Make definite plans to deal with specific worries. Then consider sharing your plans and ideas with others, especially fellow Christians who have been supportive in the past. They can give you valuable feedback about the option you have chosen. Revise your plan if necessary. Having a well-considered solution to a problem can dispel a lot of anxiety.

Incorporate into your daily routine the following "Ways to Beat Anxiety" from Philippians 4:

1. Determine to obey God, who *commands* us not to be anxious (v. 6). Notice the call to obedience. Practice a simple technique we have shared with many patients: When you catch yourself worrying, tell yourself, "Stop! Relax. Anxiety is a signal to relax, so I *will* relax."
2. Pray about your concerns (v.6).
3. Realize that God keeps your heart and mind safe when you remain obedient (v. 7). We need not "go crazy" over worries.
4. Meditate on positive thoughts (v. 8). Scripture is loaded with time-treasured thoughts you can read, ponder, and apply to your life. Take time to reflect on some of the following passages: Psalm 34:4; 86:15; Proverbs 1:33; 3:25–26; Isaiah 40:28–31; Matthew 6:33–34; 11:28–30; John 10:27–29; 14:27; Hebrews 4:15–16; 1 John 3:20; 4:10. Try to place yourself in the Scriptures you read and study.
5. Focus on godly behavior (v. 9) and avoid sin (Prov. 4:14–15).

6. Find encouragement by joining small fellowship groups (Heb. 10:24–25). Be grateful for others' concern (v. 10). And divert your attention from self to others (2:3–4). How true it is that once you get your mind off your problems by helping others, your anxiety often decreases.

7. Work on being content (v. 11; cf. 1 Tim. 6:6).

8. Recognize the "twofold responsibility" (yours and Christ's)—"I can do everything through him who gives me strength" (v. 13). Christ is the great anxiety overcomer; don't go it alone.

9. Rejoice in the Lord (v. 4), for he promises to supply all your needs (v. 19). Have you noticed that the birds are still doing quite well after all these centuries? And the flowers of the field look better than Solomon in all his royal robes. Eliminate incessant fears about poverty. God will take care of you. Mind you, he promises to supply *needs*, not *wants*. (And sometimes he even supplies the wants).

10. Realize that the grace of God is with you (v. 23; cf. 2 Cor. 9:8). Grace, unmerited favor, is the pulsebeat of salvation and the drumbeat of Christian life. Without grace, none of us could march behind the divine Drum Major. Thinking about God's unending grace relieves some of our anxieties.

Practice these practical suggestions to overcome anxiety:

Listen to music that soothes the soul (1 Sam. 16:23). Christian music, especially, can relieve stress and drive away nervousness.

Exercise regularly—ideally, three times per week.

Get adequate sleep (Ps. 127:2). Most people need eight hours of sleep per night. Depriving yourself of needed sleep is sinning against your body—the temple of the Holy Spirit.

Work recreation into your routine. Light, refreshing activity—such as sports, hobbies, or outdoor fun—can take your thoughts off worrisome circumstances.

Live one day at a time (Matt. 6:34). This attitude can be cultivated only through months of practice.

Don't procrastinate on problem-solving efforts. Putting things off causes pressure to build, leading to more anxiety. Be sure to make your plans practical and your expectations realistic.

How can I better relate to those who are grieving? What can I do to comfort them? How long does it usually take to work through the grieving process?

When Christians greet people who have just suffered a loss, they are often perplexed by what to say. As a result, they fall back on timeworn and uncomforting clichés: "Oh, but isn't it good to know he's in heaven?" or "At least she isn't suffering anymore." While statements like these may be true and even temporarily helpful, they can sound hollow, no matter how well-intentioned.

The Bible instructs us to weep with those who mourn, just as we are to rejoice with those who are glad. When friends and loved ones suffer the emotional pain of grief, they need the freedom to express that grief naturally and openly. Putting on a false acceptance of the loss is not healthy, yet clichés can spark in the survivors a feeling that it is improper to hurt as badly as they do. Suppressing grief for the sake of appearing well-adjusted and stoically resigned to tragedy can prolong the mourning period and even lead to clinical depression.

The best way to help grieving friends is with your presence. Just being there is comforting. It's not what you say that is needed; it's that you came, you stayed, you listened, you cared. They will remember little of what is said, but much of what is done.

The normal grief process includes five distinct stages, although one or more of the stages may overlap. First there is *denial,* or disbelief. The more unexpected the loss, the greater the disbelief. This period may last as little as a few moments to as much as several days (or even years in rare cases).

Next there is usually anger. "This is so unfair!" says the grieving one. This stage often includes anger toward God for "allowing" this to happen. The distorted logic of grief may even make the mourner wonder, "How could this have happened to a Christian?"

The grieving person will typically then move to *guilt* and say a lot of sentences starting with, "If only I had . . ." Some of this guilt may have some validity and need to be resolved; but most of it is false guilt prompted by the turmoil of emotional pain and sense of loss.

Once the extent of the loss settles in, *true grief* will appear, usually manifested by deep sadness and tears. This normal reaction is necessary and important. Although one does not have to be overcome with emotion to release the stress of grief, holding back feelings prolongs and worsens the pain.

Sharing the first four stages of grief with the mourners can help them reach a permanent resolution. Knowing what to expect can prepare them for the emotional struggle, but the grieving process lasts longer for some than others. How long it lasts is not as important as not getting "stuck" in one of the stages. As long as a person is consistently working through that process, grieving is normal and healthy and necessary.

If, after a long period of time, your grieving friend comes to a standstill, unable to move ahead, you can help by initiating a discussion about what he or she is feeling. In some cases the mourner may need to talk with a pastor or a professional counselor.

How can I help a Christian friend trust people? This friend wants to have better relationships, and he knows intellectually that he should trust people, but he can't bring himself to actually do it.

There is no quick way to help someone open up and allow others into his or her life. For whatever reason, lack of trust is part of your friend's personality and permeates his emotions and his mental attitudes. A good start is to slowly develop the friendship you two already share. Let him see over time that you are trustworthy. Be patient; give him your time but let him set the pace. Show him that you are a loyal friend, as you gradually become more involved in his life.

Perhaps he will come to trust you if you demonstrate your trust in him. You might request his advice, trusting him with the knowledge of your personal matters. This will likely influence him to feel more comfortable, accepted, and safe around you.

Of course, establishing a close relationship takes time; your friend needs to see that your behavior is predictable before he can begin to trust you and, eventually, others as well. He needs a model of trust so that he can learn it for himself. Let him see you as "a friend who sticks closer than a brother" (Prov. 18:24). As you reach out to him, your friend will begin to reach back. This is when the bridge of trust can finally be built.

Lack of trust in other people often reveals a greater lack of trust in God. If your friend could be confident that God would be true even when people fail him, he wouldn't be so reluctant to trust others. A lack of trust in God is often traceable to a childhood in which parents or other authority figures broke the bonds of trustworthiness.

Your friend may need specialized help from a trained Christian counselor to remove this barrier to relational living. Perhaps you should gently suggest that he take this step. You might provide him with the names of two or three reliable counselors to help point him in the right direction. In fact, you could offer to go with him to the counselor's office to give him moral support. Your friend may not want you to be present during the actual counseling session, however. Remember to be sensitive to his feelings and nonjudgmental. Unconditional love can really make a difference in your friend's life.

Finally, always remember that you cannot accept responsibility for another person's lack of trust or any other hang-ups. Just take your best shot at being a friend and realize that you've done all you can to help him.

How can I overcome my feelings of inferiority?

Feeling inferior is a complex human problem, one that most people never totally solve. We all experience times of feeling second-rate compared to others, and Satan likes to use these emotions against us.

God, on the other hand, does not want us to compare ourselves unfavorably to others. He never intended us to choose this form of false humility, nor believe such detrimental untruths about ourselves. He wants us to see ourselves as he created us, as unique individuals whose qualities are different from—but not necessarily better or worse than—anyone else's. We should, of course, feel inferior to God and look to him to provide what we cannot provide for ourselves—a remedy for sin and strength in our weakness.

The flip side of inferiority can be seen in the often unruly spirit of competition. To prove to ourselves and others that we are better than our fellowman, we sometimes strive to conquer all rivals. Society has taught us that nice guys finish second, and second means the same as last—a failure. From that perspective, unless we are first, we are embarrassed and miserable.

You can clearly see that inferiority feelings are everywhere present in the emotional struggles of daily life. While there are no quick fixes, no simple solutions, a few suggestions can put you on track to harnessing these feelings of self-doubt before they control your life.

What makes anyone "important"? The answer to that question is the foundation of dispelling inferiority feelings. Is it good looks? Intelligence? A high-paying job? An overflowing bank account? Good behavior? Personal possessions? These things may make you temporarily feel better about yourself, but none of them cures the agony of feeling unimportant. And none of them measures true personal worth.

To overcome inferiority, the Christian must learn to say and believe, "I am important because I am God's child [John 1:12] and Christ's ambassador [2 Cor. 5:20]." There is nothing *you* can do to exalt your significance. Rather, you find your worth in God's love for you, in his blueprint for your life, and in his promise of eternity. In Galatians 6:4, Paul tells us not to compare ourselves to others. Instead, Paul encourages us to be proud of ourselves for cooperating with God in our own spiritual growth (sanctification) process.

Serving God can help alleviate your feelings of inferiority. As the writer of Ecclesiastes discusses throughout the last chapter of his book of wisdom, servanthood among God's people is the only thing that brings real meaning to life. Only as time passes in your life will the correlation between joy and ministry become clear. Then the divine mystery unfolds: happiness follows after helping others.

Remember, too, there is no reason to struggle alone. The body of Christ is available to you. Seek out other believers who will love you unconditionally and support you as you strive to develop self-esteem.

Finally, read! Besides the Bible, some excellent resources have been written specifically on this theme. We suggest: *His Image, My Image* by Josh McDowell (Here's Life, 1985) and *The Sensation of Being Somebody* by Maurice Wagner (Zondervan, 1985).

I am so bitter toward my former husband. My deep anger toward him is destroying my ability to live happily. Our children's happiness is at stake, too. What can I do to get past this terrible bitterness?

You are right to realize that bitterness toward your ex-husband is destroying not only your own happiness, but also that of your children. It's good, too, that you recognize these negative feelings as "bitterness." If a person experiences hostility and unresolved tension when reviewing the past, the primary emotion involved is usually bitterness. Some people call this disturbing baggage from the past's unhappy events by other names: resentment, grumbling, jealousy or envy, inability to forgive, or grief over lost love. All these emotions are *negative* and self-defeating responses to adversity.

Hebrews 12:15 tells us: "See to it that no one misses the grace of God and that no bitter root grows up to cause trouble and defile many." We can "defile" ourselves and others with general misery, career burnout, and even psychosis (lapses from reality). When long-term anger is unresolved, it takes root in our lives and sends out shoots of bitterness. This process involves an initial feeling of anger, a decision to say nothing about the anger, and a willingness to hold on to a grudge.

The primary motive for holding a grudge is vengeance. This kind of emotional pain says, "I will not be kind or open to that person, because he [or she] deserves to suffer and does not deserve my friendship." Ironically, the other person usually does not suffer as much from our break in cordiality as we do ourselves.

The bitterness we hold inside soon manifests itself in our behavior toward others and our attitude about life in general. If the bitterness lasts long enough, an acrid personality may cope with the pain by burying it in a seeming lack of emotionality. This is depression.

The key passage to resolving bitterness is Ephesians 4:31–32:

> Let all bitterness and wrath and anger and clamor and slander be put away from you, along with all malice. And be kind one to another, tender-hearted, forgiving each other, just as God in Christ also has forgiven you (NASB).

Now you may be thinking that is easy for God to say, but that it is not so easy for you to do. A few helpful suggestions are in order:

Acknowledge that bitterness is futile, and choose to put it aside. Realize that the basic reason for holding on to your bitterness is to "get even." Then recognize that God also says that he is the only one allowed to judge and enact vengeance on your (or anyone's) behalf: "It is mine to avenge; I will repay (Deut. 32:35a). Your job is to "bless those who persecute you; bless and do not curse" (Rom. 12:14).

Express your anger appropriately, instead of trying to hold it in. Appropriate expression of anger includes confronting with respectful composure the person who is the object of your anger. Start by saying something like, "I feel [or "felt"] abandoned [or whatever] by your actions." Don't say, "You did such and such." Be specific only about your feelings, rather than presenting a list of "offenses."

A mature confrontation is not always possible, so sometimes a letter to the person who has hurt you will flush the pain out of your system, whether or not that letter is mailed. Or, if oral communication is easier for you, pretend the person is in a chair across the room from you, listening as you explain your feelings.

Speak positively to and about anyone who has hurt you. Having something positive to say can be tough, but it's worth it for your own well-being. It helps counteract the "infection" of bitterness. When your positive words are addressed directly to the person who has brought you pain, they might encourage more considerate behavior in the future.

Develop self-control. Yield your mind to Christ and let him fill it with thoughts about *his* goodness. Then thank him for any good you see in yourself or others. Depend on him to strengthen you for the battle of fighting bitterness. Without Christ, we are easily victimized by our own emotions.

Choose to forgive when wronged. This does not mean that you will always be able to forget or blot out the past and your feelings about it; but it does mean that you have identified your feelings and refuse to dwell on them. Only then will your hurts be healed. You may need to re-forgive scores of times over a period of months for a severe offense. Pray for God's help.

How can I keep from feeling so lonely? I no longer have my best friend, my husband. He died three years ago. For forty years we did everything together. I see friends at church, and my children come by to see me, but the majority of my days are filled with loneliness.

There are a number of things you can do to break the bonds of loneliness. But first you need to recognize what—beside the death of your husband—might be causing your long-term feelings of isolation. Also consider whether the "normal" grieving process has been completed. Final acceptance of a loss comes only after the stages of denial, anger, guilt, and true grief (with tears) have been resolved. (See the fourth question in this chapter.) From years of dealing with lonely patients, we have come to recognize at least five reasons for feeling cut off from the companionship of other people:

Isolation from God. It has been said that there is a "God-vacuum" in each of us. Though some may deny it, it is impossible for human companionship to fill the lonely void that only Jesus Christ was meant to fill. We can also experience isolation from God as a result of breaking fellowship with him by sin. Adam and Eve experienced this. So did King David. Without being completely aware of it, we sometimes sin by not asking for God's help and by refusing to have our loneliness cured by anything but the return of the person we have lost.

Our changing society. Our fast, mobile, and stress-filled culture tends to promote loneliness. There seems never enough time to build new relationships. Today's values emphasize excessive individualism and independence, which create a further barrier to building interpersonal connections. Television also shortens the amount of time we might otherwise devote to companionships and social activities. Research shows that excessive television watching causes individuals to be cynical and trust others less, promoting even more lonely feelings.

Rejecting others. Our staff often sees individuals who are lonely because they have rejected the overtures of others. Many people worry unnecessarily that others will not accept them, so they are unwilling to risk making new friends. It boils down to the fact that individuals frequently reject others by acting cold and aloof simply because they do not like themselves. You can't expect others to accept you as a friend if you don't accept yourself as a worthwhile individual. Become your own best friend.

Being rejected by others. Some people truly have been rejected by others. Sometimes their own attitude is to blame. For example, they may have a critical spirit, so others do not want to be around them. Or they may be the victim of circumstances—a wife feels rejected because her husband is too busy, or a Christian is rejected by a person who either spurns Christian values in general or feels uncomfortable with the former's overzealous evangelizing.

Neglect in childhood. Many children in today's society are desperately lonely because of lack of attention from a parent—a father too busy with his career or a mother trying to juggle too many roles. This may carry over to adulthood, since the child had little opportunity to learn how to build caring relationships.

In your case, as a widow of a long-term marriage, you will always miss your "best friend" and treasure the happy moments you shared. But he is gone now, and he surely would have wanted you to get back into life. There is no surefire cure for loneliness, but there are several things you can work on:

Be active. Many lonely people sit passively around, waiting for someone interesting to come along, or for something spectacular to happen. Whenever you are feeling lonely, it helps to get up and go! New activities, interests, and people all help. Join a club, take up a new hobby, do volunteer work. These may sound like simplistic solutions, but they do work. Of course, activity is only one step in the process, since many very busy people are also lonely. But give yourself a chance—don't be a stay-at-home.

Unite with others. We once knew of a lonely woman who had been in and out of psychiatric institutions for years. When she started attending church and met her pastor, he assigned two women in the church to meet with her each week for a year. That did more than any therapy had been able to do. Fellowship with others—like the other suggestions—must be combined with other parts of the "cure" for optimum benefit.

Walk closely with God. An intimate friendship with God is where the ultimate solution to loneliness really lies. The Bible tells us the story of David's returning home from battle to find that the women and children of his village had been taken captive. The homecoming warriors were bitter and lonely, but David's solution is found in 1 Samuel 30:6—"And David was greatly distressed; for the people spake of stoning him, because the soul of all the people was grieved, every man for his sons and for his daughters: but David encouraged himself in the LORD his God" (KJV).

Others find real comfort in Psalm 27:10, as did a very lonely woman who visited our clinic. She had never known her father, and her mother committed suicide. This special verse says: "Though my father and mother forsake me, the LORD will receive me." This basic step in overcoming loneliness—a close walk with God—leads to the next suggestion.

Develop the fruit of the Spirit. In Galatians 5:22–23 we read: "But the fruit of the Spirit is love, joy, peace, patience, kindness, goodness, faithfulness, meekness and self-control. Against such things there is no law." If we exhibit these beautiful qualities of acceptance, others will want to be with us. A critical and judgmental attitude will drive others away.

The fruit of the Spirit produces an overall sense of peace, which will help counteract your loneliness. Letting the indwelling Spirit control you increases your ability to be patient and forgiving. Perhaps you have unconsciously set yourself up to be lonely because of grudges you hold against certain family members and friends whom you see as having failed you. Since we are all sinful and fail others at times, holding grudges is unchristian. Besides, it is counterproductive. When the loss of a loved one brings extended loneliness, it is sometimes partly because we are angry at the loved one for leaving us, or we even blame God for having taken that person away.

Realize the love of Christ. Being grounded in God's love is probably the best remedy for any emotional problem, so accepting that love is vital for curing loneliness. But so is sharing that love with others. Offering love from a heart filled with God's love usually results in receiving more love in return. The apostle Paul prayed:

> [that] Christ may dwell in your hearts through faith. And I pray that you, being rooted and established in love, may have power, together with all the saints to grasp how wide and long and high and deep is the love of Christ, and to know this love that surpasses knowledge—that you may be filled to the measure of all the fullness of God (Eph. 3:17–19).

Dwell on your belonging to God. Even tiny infants need a sense of belonging, the assurance that their parents will never forsake them. Lonely people need to remind themselves that—as children of God—they can place all their confidence in our heavenly father. Christ promised:

> In my Father's house are many rooms. . . . I am going there to prepare a place for you. . . . I will come back and take you to be with me that you also may be where I am (John 14:1–3).

We are all eternally secure in the hands of God; we belong to him now and forever. Imaging his accepting face, despite our sinful, imperfect selves, erases our feelings of loneliness and spurs us to step out to break the solitude that sometimes surrounds us. For further help in overcoming loneliness, read Les Carter's book *Why Be Lonely?* (Baker, 1982).

Years ago my best friend confided in me that she had undergone an abortion as a teenager. I tried to convince her to put that experience behind her, but I know she has been very unhappy lately. Last week she was hospitalized with clinical depression. Could her present emotional turmoil be traced to that long-ago abortion?

Many women suffering from extreme depression are wrestling with the emotional pain of a past abortion. Years after the event they are still experiencing guilt, bitterness, anger, and despair. Such long-term effects of abortion are quite common.

Several emotions are associated with the decision to have an abortion. The first is *denial,* as a woman claims that nothing is ethically wrong with abortion. *Blame* may be passed on to others, followed by *anger* turned outward, possibly toward the man who impregnated her. Finally, *guilt* feelings and *self-hatred* are experienced. If the woman remains in this state with her emotional conflict unresolved, the inner turmoil may result in severe depression. This problem is thoroughly and expertly discussed by Terry L. Selby in his book, *The Mourning After: Help for the Postabortion Syndrome* (Baker, 1990).

Some women do not feel much remorse about having an abortion, mainly because they have denied the guilt they have buried inside. Another reason is cultural indoctrination. If we hear over and over how an unborn baby is really only "placental material," we can become desensitized to the truth—that abortion destroys a living being.

For a limited number of women, the inability to feel remorse indicates *sociopathy,* a term describing someone who is totally amoral and has rejected the laws of God and society. Since they accept no rules except their own, sociopaths answer only to themselves and will follow their every whim if they think they can get away with it.

We had one patient who had been unaware before counseling that she was plagued with guilt over two previous abortions. The abortion clinic had used misleading terms and rationalization to cover up the fact that she was taking the life of her unborn child. This woman had repressed her guilt for years but finally developed depression so severe that she became psychotic and lost complete touch with reality.

When she was admitted to the hospital, we gave her medication that stabilized her perception of reality to the point where we could counsel her. We then learned that her depression and other negative feelings started a few months after her second abortion, although she denied feeling guilty about what she had done. In further counseling we came back to that subject repeatedly. Each time, tears welled up in her eyes and she would tense up and silently fold her arms or would look away and weep uncontrollably. It took her a long while to admit to her guilty feelings. When she finally dealt with them and asked God to forgive her (and later forgave herself), she was cured of her depression.

Many women who have had an abortion feel as if neither God nor the people they care about will ever love them again. For Christian women who have asked God's forgiveness for their abortion (and any other sin), a scriptural perspective is found in Psalm 103:12:

> As far as the east is from the west, so far has he removed our transgressions from us. As a father has compassion on his children, so the LORD has compassion on those who fear him; for he knows how we are formed, he remembers that we are dust.

I have suffered great emotional pain over the abortion I had years ago. Sometimes I think I'm a terrible person who doesn't deserve to live. How can I feel better about myself?

Abortion causes *true* guilt, but Jesus took the weight of our sins on his shoulders when he died on the cross. God is not a God of punishment, but a God of love and forgiveness. He is not willing that any of his children should perish for their sins, but that all should come to repentance. When people feel that they don't even deserve to live, they need to remember that Jesus has already died for them and paid the price for their sins. They may not believe they deserve to be forgiven, but God has provided forgiveness anyway. God has graciously chosen to offer us forgiveness, and he confirmed that decision at the cross. We need only ask for it and accept our redemption.

We often punish ourselves for things we have done in the past. When Christians don't forgive themselves, they are usurping God's authority. Because God does not want vengeance, Jesus went to the cross to pay the price for our sins and remove our guilt forevermore.

You need not continue to feel guilty about your abortion. Accept God's forgiveness and then forgive yourself. Also be ready to forgive the baby's father who may have directly encouraged the abortion or abandoned you, leading you to believe you had no other recourse.

Three specific guidelines can help you resolve your painful feelings about having had an abortion:

Talk to God about your feelings. God loves you very much. He is more bighearted than anyone you will ever know. Thank God for what he said about forgiveness in Psalm 103 and 1 John 1:9. Memorize these verses and keep talking to God about them until they become meaningful to you.

Talk to a counselor. Sharing a deep, dark secret such as abortion with a counselor may uncover your buried emotions and help you deal with them more quickly. Counselors don't have all the answers, but they usually have good ears.

Deal with your feelings of guilt about the baby you lost. One woman was helped greatly by having a mock funeral for her baby. This enabled her to grieve properly. She talked to the baby and said, "I'm sorry I did that to you, and that you did not have a chance at life on this earth. I know you're in heaven, and I'll join you there someday. I ask your forgiveness." By addressing her baby directly, she was better able to release her painful emotions than if she had spoken of them only to her counselor.

Perhaps you prefer to talk mainly to God about your feelings. If so, you can ask him to tell your baby how sorry you are for not giving it an opportunity to live, and that you look forward to being reunited in eternity. This can be a tremendous release. It will make you feel better about yourself and help move you along to what lies ahead.

3

Medically Related
Emotional Distress

Many "psychological" problems have medical aspects that need to be considered and addressed along with the emotional dysfunctioning. Medical doctors who specialize in mental disorders that have organic or physiological overtones are called *psychiatrists*.

Although psychiatrists broaden their studies to include the interrelation between mental/emotional problems and physical processes, *psychologists* usually have doctoral degrees and nearly as many years of professional training as their M.D. counterparts. A psychologist is generally more educated in psychological testing and nonmedical approaches to mental health.

A *Christian* psychiatrist or psychologist adds yet another dimension to emotional problem solving by recognizing that the spiritual part of human beings plays an important role in many medical and emotional difficulties. He or she is a committed Christian and usually has had some seminary training in theology. Christian therapists view people's problems from a biblical perspective, blending medical and psychological acumen in the context of God's view of man.

While the field of psychological study has made radical advances in the last twenty years, many questions still await answers. Scores of other questions have yet to be asked, but the research continues. Modern scientific progress has been truly amazing, and curative medicines and procedures are being discovered every year. Christians should never refuse to make use of medical know-how. It is evident that many of the findings uncovered in recent years are but further proof of the complexity of God's interconnecting universe and the brilliance of his most amazing creation—the human beings meant to "have dominion" over that universe.

These thoughts are important to consider as we turn our interests toward questions that have double-edged significance in that they bear both emotional and medical implications.

I am a Christian who has been blind since birth. I'm prone to depression and have cycles of ups and downs. There are few people in my church with whom I can have fellowship. Is my blindness causing the depression, or is it related to other underlying factors?

Physical handicaps generally make people more prone to depression, reflecting the emotional struggle that often follows any type of loss. Depression feeds on our losses and turns our pain inward. A handicapped person frequently feels unfairly deprived of what *should* have been, what other people have. Because this "loss" hurts, seeing things from God's perspective requires spiritual maturity. Working through these difficult emotions can take years.

Have you tried becoming involved in a church with more people your own age? Although some churches have specific ministries to blind people and those with other handicaps, you need not limit yourself to these. Some larger churches, which you may have tended to avoid because you felt a bit overwhelmed, may offer the type of personalized ministry you want and need. Fellowshiping with people who understand your specific trials and are close to your age is important to your spiritual well-being. Joining such a congregation can dramatically enhance your emotional health.

Anyone—handicapped or not—who suffers from isolation is an ideal candidate for depression and other emotional problems. We are created as social beings, and we need each other. Sharing your own unique talents and insights in the body of Christ will help others appreciate that God's children are of equal worth. You need to realize that you have much to contribute to others!

Another avenue of help might be at hand. Many communities offer support groups of all kinds, and you may be able to find one geared specifically for your handicap. Most support groups hold regular discussion meetings and sponsor special events that attract townwide attention. You may discover a special person there to whom you can relate your feelings and frustrations. Participation in group activities will rebuild your own damaged self-esteem, give others a fresh perspective on blindness, and—above all—get you back in the mainstream of life.

You may be able to find a counselor in your area who specializes in treating people with impaired vision, but *any* experienced Christian counselor should be able to help you accept your blindness as a challenge, rather than an affliction that inevitably curtails your ability to participate fully in life.

Seek out a sighted individual with whom you can relate. Share mutual interests in music, sports, literature, or hobbies. Soon you'll be sharing thoughts and feelings. A rapport will develop. When you forget about your restriction, others will also.

Should Christians depend on medication for serious emotional problems? Shouldn't faith alone be enough to solve a Christian's problems?

Some Christians believe that antidepressant medication, for example, should never be used. Certain fringe groups even claim it is unspiritual to rely on any medical treatment whatsoever, insisting we should rely totally on the Lord. This can be likened to the attitude of a century ago, when some Christians thought it was a sin to wear eyeglasses. "Devil's eyes" they were called, the reasoning being: "If God wanted me to see well, he would have given me good vision."

Even after penicillin and other "wonder drugs" were discovered, many Christians died of curable diseases because they wanted to trust God alone for healing. Others have died because they refused to have a cancer surgically removed. They chose to believe they would be healed miraculously if they prayed hard enough and with sufficient faith.

But Christ himself implied that those who are sick need a physician (Matt. 9:12). Luke, the writer of one Gospel and the Book of Acts, was a physician (see Col. 4:14). Although it is true that God used numerous miracles of healing in the early church that gave credibility to Christianity, that does not justify the insistence that God must heal either supernaturally or not at all. It takes a grandiose person to demand a supernatural healing! Who dares to say that a given medical remedy or technique is not within the bounds of God's supernatural control or that the Almighty does not work through the extraordinary feats of modern science?

God in his perfect wisdom and superior power chooses to work within the laws he has created for humans. While *he* is not bound to those laws in any way, we cannot foolishly make demands on how God should behave. Taking life-threatening risks by refusing good medicine hardly proves super-spirituality. Some may choose to die for the cause of their pompous but distorted faith. Others choose to live totally under God's authority, which includes making use of the many effective medications he has made known to us.

God can and does heal some people supernaturally today, but most people—Christians included—are healed through the knowledgeable application of medical technology. God is at work in both forms of healing. Whatever the scenario, he makes the ultimate decisions on life and death.

Now back to a specific answer to the question. Antidepressants or other medications should be used for some emotional problems, including situations of clinical depression when a patient cannot sleep or is suicidal. For mild depressions, however, it may be better not to use expensive medications, which often have mild temporary side effects (such as dryness of the mouth and a slower reaction time).

You should certainly feel free to ask your physician about any prescribed medication you are expected to take. Why have you received the prescription and are there any unpleasant side effects? What improvement can you expect from the medication? How long will you need to take it? These are routine questions your physician should be willing and able to answer without any hesitation.

How do I know if I should go into the hospital to ease my depression? Can't counseling alone help me?

There are essentially three possible ways to treat patients with clinical depression:

1. *They can be seen in weekly therapy with no medications.* Typically, a patient so treated will recover from clinical depression within six to twelve months. A problem remaining, however, is the possibility of suicide after the first two months, sparked by extreme insomnia and unresolved emotional pain. Patients must be carefully monitored during that period.

2. *They can come for weekly psychotherapy and non-addictive antidepressants.* In this case a patient will probably overcome depression in three to nine months. Improved sleep habits will usually bring about noticeable improvement after as little as ten days. Using antidepressant medication makes suicide less of a risk than if psychotherapy is the only form of treatment. The medication increases energy level and ability to concentrate, factors which not only help the individual to return to normal productivity sooner but also increase the patient's capacity to respond more actively to therapy.

3. *They can check into the psychiatry ward of a hospital.* Here they will get daily, intensive psychotherapy and medication and usually feel better within two weeks. A typical hospitalized patient overcomes depression within three to six weeks and will usually require only a few months of follow-up outpatient visits.

Choosing a mode of treatment depends on any of a number of factors, including the severity of the symptoms and the family situation. Hospitalization may be the best option, for example, if the patient has young children at home who have been hurting for months because of a parent's depression, or if there is no other adult in the household to lend support. Likewise, hospitalization is almost always best for a depressed individual who is too depressed to function adequately at home or at work, or who is either suicidal or nearing a psychotic break with reality.

In your own case, perhaps your depression is not that severe. If you are just not functioning well, outpatient psychotherapy with medication may be the best choice for you. Since medication might shorten your recovery time, why not agree to taking it? Assuming that you have confidence in your psychiatrist and that all your questions have been answered, follow his or her professional advice on this matter.

If, on the other hand, life seems unbearable or suicidal fantasy increasingly dominates your thoughts, be sure that your therapist is aware of this. It is difficult to make major decisions during a deep depression, so before you take any action, ask for the advice of your therapist as well as close friends and family members. For severe cases of depression, hospitalization has distinct advantages:

The patient receives intensive psychotherapy, often daily.

Adjustments in medications can be made rapidly.

The patient gets away from a stressful environment and into a safe retreat with a friendly, helpful, and supportive atmosphere.

Hospital precautions help prevent suicide attempts.

Becoming acquainted with recovering patients can be a source of encouragement.

The symptoms and emotional pain of depression are cured more rapidly.

Trained psychiatric nurses and other staff members are on call to help patients gain insight into their problems. These personnel observe each patient's daily behavior patterns and relay this information to staff psychiatrists, who use it in therapy to solidify his or her progress.

Hospitalization may be less expensive than prolonged outpatient psychotherapy, which is often not covered in full by insurance.

Of course, the possible drawbacks to hospitalization should also be considered by both patient and therapist. First it should be noted that some depressed individuals try to escape responsibility for their recovery by going to a hospital and feigning or exaggerating their symptoms when a psychiatrist is around. Even when that is not the case, some social stigma is attached to psychiatric hospitalization. When patients are discharged three to six weeks after being admitted—happier, enthusiastic, and over the worst of the depression—they may find that friends are hesitant to ask questions about the hospitalization and are not fully convinced that they are "normal." A patient may take this as a personal rejection, even though it is not meant that way. Finally, without insurance, hospitalization is costly. (Even with insurance it is hardly considered ethical to run up high hospital bills unless necessary.)

What do you think about using shock therapy for depressed individuals?

Shock therapy or electroconvulsive therapy (also called ECT or EST) is used rather infrequently today because of the bad connotations associated with its use decades ago (before phenothiazine and antidepressant drugs were introduced in the early 1950s). Although some professionals still consider it an option, shock therapy or insulin coma therapy is unadvisable in our opinion, because there is potential risk to the patient, and these measures often bring only temporary relief. Even if shock therapy does cure the immediate symptoms, it will not teach the individual how to prevent becoming depressed again.

Some Christian psychiatrists do use shock therapy for severely suicidal patients or those who do not seem to be improving with antidepressant medications. They generally follow up the shock therapy with outpatient psychotherapy.

I have been feeling very depressed, and I think something is wrong with my thyroid gland. Could this have anything to do with my depression?

Thyroid disorders *can* contribute to depression, and a family physician should check a patient's thyroid function periodically. But before you attribute your feelings to thyroid problems you should make sure the depression does not originate from some other source. Ask yourself, "Is there something going on in my life that is contributing to my emotional sadness?" Or, if you grew up in a dysfunctional, broken, or unstable home, you may be carrying childhood feelings of anxiety or depression into your adult life.

When people enter the hospital under our care, checking for thyroid problems is part of the medical routine they can expect. One in twenty hospitalized patients has a thyroid disease that contributes to anxiety or depression, but these symptoms are usually not caused entirely by a malfunctioning thyroid gland. Many other underlying issues come into play, and a thyroid problem simply adds to their effect.

Hyperthyroidism (overactive thyroid) causes an "anxious" or hyperactive state, whereas *hypothyroidism* (underactive thyroid) can be a main contributor to depression. For anyone suspected of having a thyroid problem, the first step is to have certain laboratory procedures performed. Medication would be prescribed if you are found to have imbalanced thyroid activity. Then, if the depression lifts immediately, your problem would be solved.

If your thyroid activity was normal, or if your depression does not disappear after thyroid treatment, your depression is caused by something else. After tests have ruled out other physiological causes, counseling becomes the next course of action, including a careful study of your emotions in light of past experiences that may be causing the depression.

What is PMS, and why are my symptoms so severe— when other women have no such problem? Can PMS be treated?

PMS—premenstrual syndrome—is a combination of several physical and emotional symptoms whose onset is usually seven to ten days before a menstrual period. The symptoms usually cease once the menstrual flow begins. In fact, if your symptoms are lasting the entire month, PMS is not the problem. However, if your symptoms are severe, you should consult your physician for an evaluation, if you have not already done so.

PMS can be experienced as bloating (water retention), physical pains, anxiety, and/or mood changes, as well as a cluster of less common symptoms, such as food cravings, clumsiness, acne, fatigue, and inability to concentrate. One or all of these symptoms occur to some degree in as many as 50 percent of women of childbearing age. A small number have symptoms so severe that they are virtually incapacitated.

There continues to be much debate about what specifically causes PMS, but most likely a combination of organic and psychological factors is involved. Some medical experts believe it is linked to a change in norepinephrine, a brain chemical that controls moods. Others point mainly to the periodic increase in prostaglandin hormones during the menstrual cycle. Recent research has been directed toward discovering the effect of diet upon whatever chemical changes are cyclically occurring in a woman's body.

Although there are identifiable physiological aspects to PMS, the psychological component is very important. Negative emotions tend to intensify the PMS symptoms. Many women who have been hospitalized for PMS-related depression are amazed that their physical discomfort, too, decreases after they deal with emotions connected to bothersome personal issues from the past. To be sure, the PMS will probably recur, but to a much lesser degree than before counseling.

Many treatments for PMS are available, but no single treatment works for everyone. Your physician may have you try one or more of the following before you can decide which is most successful in your case:

Vitamin B6. Some doctors prescribe 100 milligrams to be taken twice a day. Although a number of women report that their PMS symptoms are alleviated greatly on this regimen, it should be tried only under a doctor's supervision. Vitamin supplements can be dangerous if used incorrectly.

Progesterone suppositories. Many women claim to feel better after using these, but research results are contradictory regarding progesterone's value in treating PMS. Some women find that their symptoms worsen with progesterone.

Antidepressants. This treatment is mainly used for patients with clinical (serious, long-lasting) depression. But a significant percentage of women say they experience relief from PMS by using the antidepressant Tofranil (generic=Imipramine).

Bromoscriptine. This drug helps minimize the breast discomfort that typically accompanies PMS.

Dietary changes. Decreasing the intake of salt, sugar, and caffeine helps decrease swelling, hypoglycemia symptoms, and the emotional agitation that often occurs before the menstrual period.

Diuretics. Some women use diuretics to alleviate bloating (edema).

Counseling. This often neglected approach to controlling PMS focuses on working through unresolved grudges from the past and relieving current emotional pressures that can increase the severity of PMS symptoms.

Addicting drugs should never be taken for PMS. Codeine has been used by some women to mask their discomfort, but addiction to any drug will lead to painful withdrawal symptoms later. Consult your family physician or gynecologist before starting any treatment, even one for which a prescription is not required. Remember, too, that biblically based counseling can never hurt—and it may be helpful for your PMS.

An excellent book on this subject has been written by a Christian gynecologist and a nutritionist. The title is *PMS: What It Is and What You Can Do About It* (Sneed and McIlhaney, Baker, 1988). You can get the book at a local bookstore or by writing directly to the publisher.

I'm twenty-five and have two young children. My husband and I are considering having one more child before choosing some permanent form of sterilization. I have mixed feelings about this. What if we decide we later want another child?

The Bible doesn't talk about sterilization and whether or not God approves of it; but it is nonetheless true that "with many advisers" plans can succeed (Prov. 15:22). Seek the counsel of those close to you. Talk to relatives and trustworthy friends, especially any who have chosen sterilization for themselves.

We have talked to hundreds on both sides of the fence. Some chose sterilization and regretted it; others were relieved by their choice. Many people are so filled with anxiety over the thought of having still another child in an already large family that they have no peace of mind until they remove that possibility. For others, pregnancy poses a serious health risk for the mother.

We believe in practical family planning but have no quarrel with those who don't share our outlook. A couple who, for whatever reason, believes that having another child is *out of the question,* sometimes decides on sterilization. However, be sure that neither of you has any reservations about this. Future changes in your life situation may later make you regret your decision.

Since ancient times, many people have based a measure of their self-worth on the ability to have children, which partially explains why infertility can cause such emotional pain. This, too, is an issue that must be thoroughly discussed. You and your husband also need to consider which of you will be least affected by the inability to parent a child. Then pray about whether God approves of having that person undergo sterilization.

Having feelings of ambivalence about sterilization is normal. Consider that some parents past the normal age for childbearing wish they could have another child or two. Because such feelings come and go, it is important to have complete information and thoroughly weigh your other options before deciding on any form of permanent sterilization. With a *tubal ligation* for a woman or a *vasectomy* for a man, some possibility exists for reversal, in the event you decide you later want another child, but this procedure is not always successful. And, of course, a vasectomy is *not* always effective—about 1 percent of men who have had vasectomies have later fathered a child. The same can be true for a woman who has had a tubal ligation, although the likelihood of failure is even less.

Throughout most of my life, I've had trouble sleeping. What exactly is insomnia, and what is the most common cause?

Insomnia is the inability to achieve a sleep pattern that will provide adequate rest. People with insomnia either cannot fall into a deep, restful sleep, or they wake up after a short time and lie sleepless the rest of the night. It can take weeks to recover from the physical effects of severe and prolonged insomnia, which can include depression of all bodily functions and dulling of the mind. Accompanying symptoms include a loss of appetite, indigestion, constipation, anemia, loss of weight, and lowered resistance to infection and disease.

Insomnia can be rooted in one or more of the following:

Anxiety or stress. Either of these underlies most cases of insomnia. This type of insomnia may be a temporary reaction to a specific worry. Once the problem is solved, normal sleep patterns usually return. However, if anxiety is generalized and prolonged, counseling may be needed to help you sort out the source of your turmoil.

Depression. This more pronounced form of anxiety/stress usually causes a characteristic disturbance in sleep, most often manifested in early morning awakening. On the other hand, some depressed people have low energy and little motivation and compensate by sleeping *too much.* Once depression is lessened during counseling, sleep disturbances generally decline but some cases may require antidepressant medication.

Age. For the most part, the need for sleep decreases with advancing age. Elderly people commonly sleep rather lightly and can be easily awakened. Generally, active adults need seven to nine hours of sleep per night, but older adults in good health require less total sleep. They may find short naps refreshing.

Stimulants. Caffeine is a major stimulant and is found in coffee, tea, certain soft drinks, and chocolate. Amounts over 600 milligrams per day, especially taken near bedtime, can cause insomnia. Specific medications—such as ulcer medicine, prescriptions for high blood pressure, and birth-control pills—can contribute to restlessness. Street drugs, especially amphetamines ("uppers"), precipitate serious sleep disturbances. Vigorous exercising or cigarette smoking near bedtime can also propagate wakefulness.

Habits and personality. Worrying about not being able to sleep can cause insomnia. If this fear becomes habitual, it may set up a chronic pattern of sleep disturbance, especially in perfectionists. Sometimes the technique of "paradoxical intention"—in which one tries to stay awake on purpose for several hours and inevitably falls asleep—is effective in abating this problem.

Sleeping conditions. Finding a comfortable position in a bed with a firm support mattress usually helps induce sleep. Remaining in one position hinders bodily relaxation. It also seems obvious enough that noise affects your ability to sleep. The bedroom should be as dark and quiet as possible, but a small night light may be comforting and not disturb your rest.

General physical condition and pain. Headaches, muscle pain, upset stomach, allergies, and other medical disorders (thyroid disease, seizures, hypoglycemia, and cerebrovascular disease) often interrupt normal sleep patterns.

Specific disorders. Certain conditions, such as *sleep apnea* (temporary cessation of breathing) not only interfere with sleep but can be life-threatening. *Nocturnal myoclonus* (involuntary jerking of legs) and another condition called "restless legs" are equally bothersome to normal sleep, as are *narcolepsy,* nightmares, talking in one's sleep, teeth grinding, sleepwalking, and bedwetting. If any of these problems is suspected, a doctor should be consulted, since some problems can be overcome with behavior modification and/or medication.

Irregular routine. Going to bed and getting up at different hours from one day to the next will usually disturb sleep patterns. The body tries to adjust to sleeping within a certain time frame. Each individual is different, so a sleep schedule should be planned according to personal needs and preferences.

Listed below are several suggestions to help you improve your sleep habits so that you get the rest your body needs to function at its optimum level. (For a comprehensive look at normal sleep and sleep disturbances, read our book, *Sweet Dreams, A Guide to Productive Sleep,* [Grand Rapids: Baker, 1985]).

12 Steps to Overcoming Sleep Disorders

1. Realize that you are not alone. Surveys indicate that one-third of Americans have problems sleeping. People over 65 are six times more likely to have trouble with sleep than those age 45 or younger.
2. Obtain a thorough medical evaluation of your problem. There are basically three types of sleep disorders:

dysomnia, or "normal" restlessness brought on by stress; *hypersomnia* (daytime sleepiness, narcolepsy, sleep attacks during the day, sleep drunkenness); and *parasomnia,* or abnormal events during sleep (nightmares, sleep terror disorders, sleepwalking).

3. Have a professional evaluate whether you have underlying psychological problems that need treatment (e.g., depression, boredom, anxiety disorder).

4. Obtain treatment for any underlying medical disorders that may be provoking sleep trouble (e.g., sleep apnea, "restless legs" syndrome, arthritis, Alzheimer's, hyperthyroidism, angina, high blood pressure, chronic headaches, diabetes).

5. Avoid the use of any substances that could be causing insomnia (e.g., caffeine, nicotine, Sansert, thyroid, steroids, Aldomet, Theodur, anti-arrhythmic agents). *However, do not discontinue any prescription drugs without consulting your physician.*

6. Keep a sleep diary. Record when you go to bed, about when you fell asleep, how many times you awakened in the night, what awakened you (if you can tell), the time of each awakening, and when you awakened to start the next day. Calculate your average daily sleep time by adding to nighttime hours any daytime naps (or sleeping in front of the television set!). Perhaps you can stop worrying about how much sleep you are getting if the total approximates the normal requirement.

7. Use non-pharmacological treatments. That is, avoid the use of "sleep medications." Education yourself about sleep disorders, decrease your intake of fluids, try to avoid daytime naps, exercise early in the day, manage illnesses that affect your sleep, regulate your sleep schedule, and try "progressive relaxation" (a technique in which you gradually relax all your muscles by visualizing every part of your body from head to toe in sequence).

8. Optimize your sleep environment (i.e., temperature, light, noise, mattress). Make the bedroom a place of intimacy and rest.
9. Use common sense. Go to bed only when sleepy. Then, if you don't fall asleep in 20 minutes, get out of bed and do some nonarousing activity (e.g., read, knit, listen to quiet music). Return to bed only when you become really sleepy again.
10. Consider changing your lifestyle. Practice being more physically active during the day. Take time for joyful living. Have a light snack at bedtime, excluding high protein. Try to avoid problem-solving or controversy before bedtime.
11. Ask your doctor if you can discontinue the use of medications on a short-term basis (especially L-Tryptophane, chlorohydrate, antihistamines, and minor tranquilizers). *Always consult your physician first.*
12. Read Scripture. Studying God's Word has a cleansing and soothing effect on the mind and soul—and the devil will do his best to give you excuses for not doing so! For example, test the Psalms tonight, and see if they don't carry you off into pleasant dreams. An added benefit is that your knowledge of God's Word will accelerate over time, because your subconscious will be at work through the night, storing what you read. Thousands of years ago God inspired Job to write:

> In a dream, in a vision of the night, when deep sleep falls upon men, while slumbering on their bed, Then He opens the ears of men, and seals their instruction (Job 33:15, 16 NKJV).

King David also wrote,

> "I will bless the LORD who has given me counsel; My heart also instructs me in the night seasons (Ps. 16:7 NKJV).

4

Love, Marriage, and Family Stability

Various studies indicate that as many as 50 percent of marriages taking place today will end in divorce. This includes a significant number of Christian marriages. Close to half the children in today's society will grow up with only one parent (with or without the influence of a stepparent) or in a shared-custody arrangement. This leads to complicated family dynamics, bringing confusion to the lives of many young people that is often carried into adulthood. There are biblical and common-sense methods of preserving marital harmony—forestalling trouble before it begins and, if that fails, repairing differences before they become serious.

The questions and answers in this section examine marriage from the perspectives of compatibility, expectation levels, the importance of trust, pressures on home life, how to "fight fair," and practicing "tough love" in a family unit.

Many people divorce because they claim to be "incompatible" with their mate. Are certain personality types more likely than others to get along? How can I avoid marrying the "wrong" person?

It is impossible to marry the "wrong" personality type, since any two types can get along if both people are committed to Christ and to each other and are willing to work at strengthening their relationship. "Marital incompatibility" per se simply doesn't exist; it is a man-made term devised to provide an easy way out of an unpleasant relationship. Any two people willing to commit themselves to Christ and to each other can have a happy marriage if they are willing to work at it. Yet, incompatibility is the leading complaint among patients who are looking for someone else to blame for their problems. Patients suffering from severe depression often claim that their mates are so "perfectionistic" or "overly emotional" that it has caused their state of despair.

It is true, however, that differences in personality can cause serious conflict in a marriage. One common example is found when an *obsessive* marries a *histrionic*. The fun-loving, highly emotional person often wants to marry someone who is more stable, who will take care of the bills and make sure other details are managed. For this reason a histrionic gravitates toward obsessive-compulsives.

On the other hand, an obsessive-compulsive is often attracted to someone who is more volatile and flexible. The obsessive, although conscientious, responsible, and the possessor of many positive attributes, often lacks spontaneity and the ability to cut loose, laugh, have fun, and be aware of personal feelings. American society has tended to prize marriages between "emotional" women and seemingly "stronger" men, although this idea is changing. Obsessive women are also often attracted to emotional, histrionic males.

Whereas obsessives often lack sensitivity, histrionics are sometimes deficient in the area of judgment. They are mutually attracted because they counterbalance each other's weaknesses. But the very fact that they do approach life differently can lead to misunderstandings.

One of the toughest marital combinations is *compulsive* with *compulsive*. Although the partners have so many traits in common, both are so picky that they constantly try to control each other and will argue over such trivial details as what temperature to set the thermostat. If both are patient, mature, and conscientious, however, they can serve the Lord well in a fulfilling relationship.

A best combination in marriage doesn't exist. A good marriage depends largely on maturity. How tolerant are the partners? How flexible? Can they settle disputes rationally? Do they know how to communicate? No two people, especially Christians, should passively settle for marital unhappiness, since they have the power to make it better. A first step is learning to accept the other's personality as a given—unconditionally—without demanding any change from the mate. Each mate has an equal responsibility for making the marriage work.

It is especially important not to displace negative emotions from the past onto each other. One partner may be very angry about something that happened years ago and take it out on the other, not realizing that it is really an unresolved conflict, often dating from childhood. Such conflicts should be settled personally, within the *shelter* of marriage but not at the expense of one's partner.

Most people don't significantly change their basic personality traits after their sixth birthday. Psychological research and Scripture confirm, however, that change in behavior and attitude is possible. Yet most people are willing to allow their personality to control them—to remain "victims" of their genes and family upbringing. Only a rare few ever try to change completely; others pick and choose among undeveloped traits and try to incorporate them into their lives for self-improvement.

It is not necessary to change your *basic* personality type. But you can adapt to it. You can do all things through Christ who strengthens you (Phil. 4:13)—and that includes overhauling your personality, polishing the positive qualities that define you as a person.

Simple modifications often make a big difference. What most of us need is not an entire change in personality, but rather an effort to become more Christlike in the personality we already have. God used the histrionic Peter to accomplish certain things; and he used the obsessive-compulsive apostle Paul to achieve other things. He even used the passive-aggressive Timothy. God can use *anybody*, regardless of personality type or traits, provided that person submits to divine authority and aims for personal balance.

Romans 8:29 says that God's goal in each of our lives is greater Christlikeness: "For those God foreknew he also predestined to be conformed to the likeness of his Son." In everything we do, God wants us to be more like Christ, while retaining our own unique differences.

What is "unhealthy" love?

This term refers to an addictive attraction that focuses on one's own needs. Since it is a selfish "love" that essentially places demands on the other person in the relationship, it is certainly not *Christian* love. Such a stifling relationship is often the by-product of an affection-starved childhood; as an adult the person obsessively seeks affirmation and "proof" that he or she is loved.

By adulthood one should have learned what it means to have self-esteem and become aware of the tremendous love God has for all his children. This can be a real anchor for life. Healthy self-love starts with an understanding of God's unconditional love and enables a person to erase the unhealthy, stringent demands for love from other people. Instead of obsessively craving love, he or she begins to see the importance of a give-and-take intimate relationship, including what it means to have healthy desire.

Who hasn't read romantic fairytales about people who fall

in love and live happily ever after? Yet divorce is commonplace, Christian marriages not excluded. This is both unfortunate and avoidable; through activating one's faith in Christ, imperfect but quite "happily-ever-after" marriages are possible and healthy love becomes the norm.

One form of "unhealthy" love is *co-dependency*, a term currently in vogue in the media and usually referring to a relationship in which one person's total orientation is toward securing the comfort and approval of a loved one. Such a situation is commonly seen in homes where one family member has serious coping problems and/or is an alcohol or drug abuser. Co-dependents have lost the ability to function as individuals. Instead of facing up to the loved one's unacceptable behavior and concentrating on their own problems, co-dependent family members are in a constant struggle to "keep the peace" at any cost. In its extreme form, these victims of addictive love are co-conspirators. They perpetuate the beloved's negative acts and attitudes by going to great lengths to excuse, condone, and enable them, often to the detriment of their own well-being. This type of scenario explains why some abused spouses remain for years in an unsafe and unhealthy marriage and why families of alcoholics unwittingly reinforce the latter's excess drinking rather than confronting the problem directly.

Unconditional love implies that we are to forgive others for their shortcomings, but not that we self-destruct in the process. Our primary allegiance must be to God, since only he is worthy of our complete and absolute dependency, confidence, and trust. When our lives are centered on Christ, wholesome human relationships will develop as well.

Addictive, obsessive love results from being *overly* dependent on another person. We all have legitimate dependency needs, and God meant us to be interrelated with our fellow beings. For example, he likens Christians to the interdependent parts of a human body: "The eye cannot say to the hand, 'I don't need you!' And the head cannot say to the feet, 'I don't need you!'" (1 Cor. 12:21). The problem here is that some people do not know how to meet their needs for dependency in healthy ways. Human companionship helps fulfill these needs. However, when people who are unsure of their own worth fear rejection, they don't get close to others, which causes their dependency needs to increase all the more. Because loneliness and depression commonly complicate the lives of people who are only able to love addictively and demandingly, they often settle for an unhealthy relationship, blindly expecting one person to meet all their needs.

Those who love addictively must learn to deal with their exaggerated dependency by changing their old pattern of doing things. For example, they must learn that friendship begins with openness, a sharing of self, and a willingness to accept others (and themselves) as they are. Gradually they will recognize their own self-worth, and others will respond with warmth and affection.

Some try to deny their need for other people by going to the opposite extreme—becoming completely independent. They attempt to become "super-persons" and "super-helpers" of others. Such people often feel that showing how caring and helpful they are proves they need no one to take care of them. Of course, this is a defense mechanism. Denying all their own needs and trying to compensate by becoming magnanimous caregivers gives them a certain amount of fulfillment and may earn them expressions of gratitude that may or may not connote affection. But they become dependent on the need to be needed. Rather than stop helping others, these people must realize they are headed for burnout and begin to reorder their lives toward balance. Real love involves both giving *and* receiving.

What is healthy love?

There is no better description of what love is meant to be—and what it is *not*—than the famous love passage, 1 Corinthians 13.

Love is patient. An attitude of acceptance toward others is the cornerstone of real love. Setting rigid expectations for a relationship only leads to frustration. If we let God take care of the expectations, handling wrongs and disappointments will be easier. It also lets us praise God for the kindnesses we do receive, instead of just expecting them as our entitlement.

Love is kind. Insensitivity, sarcasm, and thoughtlessness chip away at the foundation of love. These "termites" do their work subtly, but the damage can be extensive. Love that thrives is warm-spirited and helpful. Where kindness abounds, love blossoms freely.

Love is not envious. Wanting what belongs to others has no part in love. True love celebrates a loved one's successes and never wishes to pirate the accolades of another.

Love is not proud or boastful. Love is rich in humility and poor in arrogance. Puffed-up conceit has no place in a loving relationship.

Love is not rude. Rudeness is a put-down and signifies rejection. Love is about sensitivity and acceptance. A loving person is polite and considerate and never runs roughshod over the feelings of others.

Love is not selfish. Self-centeredness is an evidence of wrong priorities. Shouldn't God be first? Egocentricity damages relationships and eventually drives away the very people we claim to love.

Love is not easily provoked. An intolerant, chip-on-the-shoulder attitude is demanding and full of anger. All of us can be irritated at times, but a commitment to love takes aggravation in stride.

Love keeps no record of wrongs. If you have genuine love, you don't keep a score card that tallies past grievances. Resist the temptation to drag out things that should have been long buried and forgotten.

If God can forgive and forget, who are we to hold grudges? Let every day be fresh and new.

Love rejoices in truth and despises iniquity. Using other people's evil to excuse our own sin damages our capacity to love. Only when truth is held in highest regard and integrity guides our actions is genuine love being expressed.

Love is protective. Love means never attacking another person's character by calling names and speaking carelessly. If a loved one makes a mistake or disappoints us, we are to find a polite way of talking and dealing with the anger we feel. It is love that ultimately protects a relationship and keeps us willing to work toward positive measures for correction. We can nurture love by praying together about any problem that threatens our commitment to each other.

Love is trusting and persevering. The word *hope* is all-important to love. An attitude that gives up when problems arise crushes a relationship. Love is optimistic because it believes that God has a plan. Love never fails if it says, "Lord, help us, and we will find a solution together."

Take a close look at the type of love you are showing for others, and see if you need to exchange some addictive patterns of love for more healthy types of affection. One of the greatest needs in America today is for strong Christian homes. Young people need examples of happy marriages, where husband and wife work at building their love, where problems are solved politely, and where children are cherished and disciplined in love. (A helpful book that examines communication in marriage is *Family Foundations* by Paul and Richard Meier [Baker, 1981].)

I had such high hopes for my marriage and expected my husband to make me happy forever. But now he constantly disappoints me, and we seem to be arguing about

everything. Although I think my suggestions and requests are quite reasonable, he says I am too demanding. How can I get through to him?

Perhaps your question is better phrased as "How can we get through to each other?" Even if, when you married, the two of you were deeply in love and firmly committed to each other, it was unreasonable to anticipate that there would never be disagreements. By hoping that your husband would *make* you happy, you were essentially putting him in charge of your level of contentment. No one person can completely satisfy another's needs or fulfill his or her every desire.

Of course, there are certain standards that must be rigorously upheld in any healthy marriage, most notably complete fidelity and freedom from physical or emotional abuse. Beyond that, however, most people expect entirely too much from a spouse. When a newlywed's blinders are removed in the ups and downs of daily life, he or she comes to realize that the beloved is—like all humans—fallible and imperfect. Clinging unrealistically to ideas about how a partner should change for "the better" (however defined) invites disillusionment, bitterness, and even depression. If you have truly accepted your husband "for better or worse," you will silently acknowledge his faults and your own and adjust your expectations accordingly. Being open about your feelings makes you able to recognize how you differ as individuals, which is the first step in working together for your mutual benefit and happiness.

Only the Lord can bring about a change in a person. If you must set high expectations, set them only for yourself. Being a model of Christlikeness for your husband can be the turning point that leads to a change in his behavior, but only if that "change" reflects God's standards, not merely your own. In any event, it will help relieve your frustrations regarding the relationship.

If your mate agrees to do something you "expect,"

don't hold unreasonable hope that he will come through for you. Furthermore, don't harp on failures to perform as promised. Without bitterness or nagging, leave the matter to your spouse. If an important deadline is involved, you might have to make sure the project gets finished (e.g., bills paid or finances reconciled). In such cases, share your disappointment in your mate's "forgetfulness" by something like, "I'm feeling angry because you promised to do this by today and I had to do it myself. I love and forgive you, but I wish I had been able to depend on you."

Remember, it's not a sin to get angry with someone, as long as you verbalize your feelings to that person and forgive as soon as possible—don't let your anger and disappointment build into bitterness. Work hard to be forgiving and pray that God will help you recognize your own imperfections and deal with the faults of others.

What with choir practice, Bible study, and prayer groups, I seem to have less and less time for my family. How can I be sure that my children are learning Christian principles?

Even today, when there is increasing emphasis on the importance of family life, some Christians continue to misinterpret the scriptural command to place God "first" in their lives. Well-intentioned though they may be, they unwittingly neglect their parental responsibilities by working day and night for the Lord and his church. This is an outright contradiction of our Bible-based accountability for the welfare of our children.

Fortunately that trend is being reversed, and other religious and secular authorities increasingly recognize that family life is foundational to a healthy society. For example, Dr. James Dobson and his "Focus on the Family" ministry has had a tremendous impact on how Christians and non-Christians alike value the home. He stresses that the biblical call to "turn the hearts of the fathers to their children, and the hearts of the children to their fathers" (Mal. 4:6) is more urgent than ever.

A number of years ago, Paul Meier's research on successful families revealed that they all included five factors. (These traits are given in greater detail in his book *Christian Childrearing and Personality Development* [Baker, 1977]).

1. *Love.* When there is genuine love, we want what is best for another person without expecting anything in return. If we are nice to a spouse or a child so that he or she will be nice to us, that is not love. It is selfishness in disguise. Love means trying to make the lives of others better each day simply out of a kind heart. Unless we have recognized and experienced God's love, we humans have very little true love to give. Love is not a commodity to be traded, as in "I'll scratch your back and you scratch mine." Only through Christ can we have and give real love.

2. *Discipline.* Both the Bible and psychological research maintain that if you are not willing to discipline your children, then you don't really love them. Too many moms and dads say, "We just love him too much to spank him." The truth is they don't understand the importance of careful discipline and that it doesn't always have to be *physical.*

Babies are born self-centered and demanding. Discipline helps correct that. Proverbs 29:15 says, "The rod of correction imparts wisdom, but a child left to himself disgraces his mother." God shows his love for his children by chastising us when we need it. So, too, must human parents "train a child in the way he should go" (Prov. 22:6).

Be clear on this, however: In no wise does God approve of injuring another, much less a child. Abuse of any nature is reprehensible—God hates it. Many forms of discipline are available apart from spanking. Above all, realize that discipline is meant to teach, not to punish. If your discipline amounts to only penalizing for wrongdoing, it comes short of what God wants from you as a parent.

In situations when spanking seems the best choice of

discipline, never strike out of anger. Compose yourself. Spank only the child's bottom—the spot least likely to suffer any physical damage. (A newspaper is useful for discipline because it doesn't really hurt, but the sound it makes is awesome and memorable.) Spanking may be justifiable for young children in open rebellion, but if they are doing something wrong and are not aware of it, teach them what is right. Remember, children make mistakes and have "accidents"; such things don't warrant spanking. Use alternative forms of discipline beginning in pre-puberty—ages ten to twelve. By age thirteen, spanking is inappropriate.

Incidentally, physical abuse is a crime, and it deserves punishment. Children are a heritage from God, and they should be cherished. If you know a child is suffering mistreatment, it is your civic obligation to report it to the proper authorities.

Finally, and most importantly, even when disciplinary measures are enacted, reinforce your expressions of love for your child. Discipline is taxing on children. Don't let it cause them confusion about how much you value them.

3. *Consistency.* Parents need to be consistent with their children and in accord about what is acceptable behavior. Usually one parent tends to be more lenient than the other, but you should avoid disagreeing on discipline in front of the children. Instead, talk about your differences privately and present your decision to the children later. Otherwise, they will try to manipulate you. If one parent says "No" to something, a child may learn to go to the other parent to try to get a "Yes." Present a united front. Work out a compromise before you discuss house rules and discipline with your children.

4. *Good examples.* Realize that children are better at imitation than obedience. They will do what you *do* before they do what you say. Children don't always listen to what parents say, but they do follow their parents' example.

Generally, boys model more after Dad and girls more

after Mom, but children pick up behavior patterns and attitudes from both parents. If there is no Dad, or if he is gone most of the time, both the boys and girls will model themselves after Mom unless there is an appropriate "surrogate" father figure. Sometimes boys in an all-female environment exhibit homosexual tendencies as they grow older. Girls in an all-female environment tend to crave male attention and often become promiscuous. Both parents are needed at home, and kids are entitled to their quantity and quality time from birth on. About half of our behavioral traits are formed by the time we are three years old. By age six, about 85 percent of our habits and attitudes have been established. After this, most people are too set in their ways for change to be probable without a whole lot of work. Parents are the most influential role models, and unfortunately they do not always set the best example.

5. *Male leadership in the home.* This is a controversial subject today. The apostle Paul said, "Wives, submit to your husbands as to the Lord. For the husband is the head of the wife as Christ is the head of the church, his body, of which he is the Savior. Now as the church submits to Christ, so also the wives should submit to their husbands in everything" (Eph. 5:22–24). But then the passage goes on to say: "Husbands, love your wives, just as Christ loved the church and gave himself up for her to make her holy. . . . husbands ought to love their wives as their own bodies" (vv. 25, 28a). Although a number of passages teach that the man should be head of the home, such a position is acceptable only if underscored by a sacrificial love that focuses on the welfare of the wife.

In the biblically commanded "one flesh" relationship, the husband is not a dominating tyrant. Rather, he is to provide unwavering leadership for the family. The crux of the family's success is on his shoulders. Both husband and wife are of equal importance in the home, but God holds the man ultimately responsible for leadership. Marriage partners should make decisions together, with mutual submission to each other's respective abilities. "Submit to one another out of reverence for Christ" (Eph. 5:21).

If, after discussing their differences, husband and wife still disagree, someone must be responsible for the decision. God says that someone is the husband. Whether or not he takes this responsibility, God holds him accountable for the results. Only when a husband's final decision blatantly disagrees with Scripture should a wife refuse to follow it.

Those are the five basic characteristics of mentally and spiritually healthy homes. A few other important considerations might be added to this list:

Put careers after family. Mothers sometimes *have* to work outside the home, but some people are not motivated by necessity alone. Placing your baby in a day-care situation simply to have more material goods or find personal "fulfillment" is not wise. Children are much more important than possessions or recognition. You have a lifetime to build a career, but only a limited number of years to enjoy your children and raise them to be responsible adults.

Don't even use the excuse that "we both have to work to meet the house payment." Children are better off living in a small house with parental supervision than in a mansion with both parents gone much of the time. Sometimes it seems that a fancy home, a second car, or some other luxury is something the devil holds up in front of parents like a carrot held in front of a donkey. Allowing your children to grow up in a day-care center can have some far-reaching effects you may spend a lifetime regretting. Don't deprive them of your nurture and influence unless you absolutely must—and be sure that a "must" is not actually merely a "want."

Don't burn out at church. Christians should not volunteer endlessly for jobs in the church when those jobs impinge on their time at home with their families. Do one job in the church well, also remembering that good parenting is also a fruitful ministry for Christ.

My wife has left me and taken our children with her. I want to win her back because I'm committed to our marriage, but she has returned to a sinful lifestyle. She seems very angry and bitter when I call and want to reconcile, so I've been avoiding her. Where do I go from here?

Dr. James Dobson talks about an unusual application of love in his book *Love Must Be Tough.* Be careful not to assume, however, that *you* are the righteous one and your mate is the one who needs "tough love." Believing in our own blamelessness is an instinct of human nature. We all tend to think we are right and the other person is wrong. Perhaps you need to practice "tough love" in this situation, but not until you understand and accept your part in the marriage's failure.

With this in mind, first try to keep the lines of communication open. Avoiding your wife may ease the pressure you feel, but meanwhile the two of you will drift even farther apart. Also, consider the following ideas:

Warmth sometimes wins people. Alienated people can be reached sometimes through sincere warmth. Your wife's quick return to a sinful lifestyle suggests that she is trying to find acceptance that you may or may not have provided in the past. All humans have a deep craving to love and to be loved. Adults from dysfunctional families have stronger than normal cravings for love, attention, and significance. Such people often confuse sex with love and acceptance. Winning your wife back may take warmth and kindness, perhaps flowers and other tangible expressions of your thoughtfulness. "Proof" of your love is probably very important to her. And you must accept the possibility that she may never come back, no matter what you do.

Make changes of your own. Some people are convinced that theirs is the only way of seeing things. If that is your disposition, don't be fooled by any rigid tendencies in your personality. Your wife may have some serious sin problems, but this should not be the main focus of your attention for now. You must come to see the personality traits that you add to the conflict and then take steps to change and grow, whether or not your wife ever comes back.

Support groups can help. If your wife is a Christian, encourage her to get into a church-affiliated support group. Group interaction helps many people see their problems more objectively. This can ignite her growth in Christ, which will in turn enable her to deal with the sin weaknesses you mentioned. (You, too, might benefit from joining such a group.)

If she is into alcoholism or drug abuse, she may need more than routine help; she may even need to be hospitalized. A Christian-oriented psychiatric unit provides counseling seven days a week and usually produces more rapid results for believers than secular facilities.

Joint counseling may be needed. Your marriage may not have much hope unless the two of you go together to your minister for spiritual counseling. Pastors who are well-trained and experienced as counselors can be effective mediators in cases of marital conflict. In practicing "tough love," you might say to your wife, "I'm willing to take you back if you agree to go with me for counseling every week, for however long it takes to save our marriage. I'm willing to learn what I need to do to change, and I hope you're equally willing." If your pastor does not have time to do long-term marital counseling, he or she should be able to recommend an alternate counselor.

Forgiveness is essential. Whether or not your wife changes, it is vital for you to forgive her, or you will likely become increasingly angry. As your anger turns into bitterness, you may become filled with thoughts of revenge. Bitterness and revenge are counterproductive and are also leading causes of depression. If reconciliation is not possible, and your wife divorces you, continue seeing your pastor to help you work through your grief and anger.

Since your children are undoubtedly suffering already from the sudden changes in their lives, they probably should have counseling, too. If they are angry or sad or have other negative feelings, they need to talk those things out and learn about forgiveness. Try calmly to convince your estranged wife to see that the children receive this guidance. In the event of a divorce, even if your wife is granted custody, you may need to make sure they receive proper counseling for as long as necessary.

Other books that offer good advice for people in your situation include *The Push-Pull Marriage* by Les Carter (Baker, 1983), and *Family Foundations* by Drs. Richard and Paul Meier (Baker, 1981), which has a section on "24 Guidelines for 'Fighting Fair' in Marriage." (See answer on pages 78–80, which lists these guidelines.)

My husband is a Christian but recently has returned to his old sinful ways. He often comes home late and lies to me about where he has been. This brings back memories of the heartaches we had before he became a Christian. How can I deal with my feelings of distrust, especially since he gets so angry when I question him?

It may be wise *not* to trust him, and to tell him so! You can express this by saying, "You've obviously lied to me about several things, and I've caught you in those lies. It would be foolish of me to believe you now. When I do catch you in a lie, I'm going to confront you with it. When I get angry with you, I'm going to tell you so. I'll draw the line on your unacceptable behavior, but I'll do my best to be the kind of wife God wants me to be."

Make your husband understand that if he ever wants you to trust him again, he will have to rebuild your belief in him with long-standing behavioral changes. If, after a year or two, he seems to have mended his ways and is still growing in the Lord, you can begin to trust him again. When you first confront him, he may "repent," even with tears. That's fine, but it will take a year or two to rebuild your trust.

Your distrust is healthy, because it means you are being

realistic. If you had trusted him blindly, self-deception would have destroyed you from the inside—deep down the truth would have eaten away at you. You must face the problem squarely and work through it one step at a time.

As was discussed in the previous question, "tough love" may be the correct way to go, especially if your husband has unresolved sociopathic tendencies. We're all born egotistical and demanding, but—through growing in the Lord, discipline in childhood, receiving lots of love, and having good role models—our self-centeredness fades into the recesses of our personality.

Sociopaths often explode with anger when they don't get what they want. If someone interrupts their sinfulness, they will direct their rage at the person who is confronting them. Antisocial behavior, at whatever level, is the hallmark of the sociopath; and the essence of that behavior is rejection of the imposed, unwelcome demands of individuals and society itself. Do not counter his anger with an emotional outburst of your own. Refuse to be drawn into a shouting match, but let him know that you are willing to discuss the matter when he is calm. Most importantly, retreat if his level of anger threatens to erupt into physical violence.

Your patience affords you the right to know where he's going and what he's doing when he "comes home late." It is very much within the bounds of fairness for you to say, "Honey, I hope you're being faithful to me. I have no respect for infidelity, and I certainly don't want to run the risk of coming into contact with a sexual disease. As your wife I have the right to know the truth about what is happening in your life." Be up front with him with such comments as: "If you want to be married to me, then you need to be faithful. If you're not going to be faithful, maybe you should consider your other options and decide to leave."

Don't automatically assume that your husband has committed adultery. Every man experiences struggles of sexual temptation, especially when troubled by other problems. This may be what your husband is going through, and he really needs your understanding. Encourage him to share these struggles with you and with a couple of close male friends. Talking over his feelings may lessen the likelihood of his actually acting on them.

If your husband is involved in pornography, for example, he might be too embarrassed to talk to you about it, and this could certainly affect your sexual relationship. Ask him to think about talking to a pastor or other Christian counselor or a loyal friend. Offer to attend counseling with him. A wise counselor can teach you both how to express your negative emotions, how to empathize with the struggles a man experiences over his sexuality, and how to improve your mutual enjoyment of marital intimacy, if that has also been a problem.

My husband and I seem to be constantly fighting but never really resolve our problems. While the fights are often over trivial matters, we still become very angry. We love each other and are both committed to the marriage. What can we do to stop the fighting?

Any couple (or individual) who is having difficulty handling emotions evoked by the stresses of everyday life should seek counseling from a qualified professional. All married people argue from time to time, so it's unrealistic not to expect some fighting to occur. The important factor is how these disagreements are handled. Love and fair play must predominate in any worthwhile relationship, even during these times of stress and disagreement. The goal should not be to determine a "winner," but to reach a satisfactory solution for all concerned, with a minimum of emotional pain.

In their book *Family Foundations: How to Have a Happy Home* (Baker, 1981), Drs. Paul and Richard Meier present "24 Guidelines for 'Fighting Fair' in Marriage," which can be very helpful in learning how to disagree *positively.* Before you start practicing these ideas, keep in mind two basic principles. First, be sure you accept your mate unconditionally; decide to love him despite his minor flaws, whether or not he changes. Second, choose happiness and peace for yourself by determining to practice the "fighting fair" guidelines, even if your husband does not.

24 Guidelines for "Fighting Fair" in Marriage

1. Sincerely commit your lives to Jesus Christ as Lord.
2. Consider marriage a lifelong commitment, just as Christ is eternally committed to his bride, the church.
3. Agree to always listen to each other's feelings, even if you disagree with the appropriateness of those feelings.
4. Commit yourselves to both honesty and acceptance.
5. Determine to attempt to love each other unconditionally, with each partner assuming 100 percent of the responsibility for resolving marital conflicts. (The 50–50 concept seldom works!)
6. Consider all the factors in a conflict before bringing it up with your mate.
7. Confess to Christ any personal sin in the conflict before confronting your mate.
8. Limit the conflict to the here and now. Never bring up past failures, since they should all have been forgiven long ago.
9. Eliminate the following phrases from your vocabulary: "You never" or "You always"; "I can't" (instead substitute "I won't"); "I'll try" (usually means "I'll make a halfhearted effort but won't quite succeed); "You should" or "You shouldn't" (which are parent-to-child statements).
10. Limit the discussion to the one issue that is the center of the conflict.
11. Focus on that issue rather than attacking each other.
12. Ask your mate if he or she would like some time to

think about the conflict before discussing it—but never put it off past bedtime. (See Eph. 4:26.)

13. Each mate should use "I feel . . ." messages, expressing a *response* to whatever words or behavior aroused the conflict. For example, "I feel angry toward you for coming home late for supper without calling me first" is an adult-to-adult message, whereas "You should always call me when you're going to be late for supper" is a parent-to-child message. These are demanding and will put your mate on the defensive.

14. Never say anything derogatory about your mate's personality. (Proverbs 11:12 tells us that someone who "derides his neighbor" lacks judgment.)

15. Even though your mate won't always be justified in reproving you, recognize him or her as an instrument of God, working in your life. Proverbs 12:1 says that "he who hates correction is stupid."

16. Never counterattack, even if your mate does not follow these guidelines.

17. Don't tell your mate why you think he or she does certain things (unless asked), just stick to your feelings on the matter. Feelings can be inappropriate to a given situation, but they *are* your feelings nonetheless. As someone has said, "Perception is as important as reality."

18. Don't try to read your mate's mind. If you're not sure what was meant by something that was said, ask for clarification.

19. Commit to following carefully the instructions given for married couples in the Bible (see Eph. 4; 1 Cor. 13). This will help you avoid becoming depressed and discouraged, which only increases irritability and worsens marital conflicts.

20. Be honest about your true emotions, but keep them under control. Proverbs 15:18 says, "A hot-tempered man stirs up dissension, but a patient man calms a quarrel."

21. Remember that the resolution of the conflict is what is important, not who wins or loses. If the conflict is resolved, you *both* win. You are teammates, not competitors.

22. Agree with each other on what topics are "out of bounds" because they are too hurtful or have already been discussed (for example, in-laws, long-term obesity, and so on).

23. Pray about each conflict before discussing it with your mate.

24. Commit yourselves to learning and practicing these guidelines. Agree to call "foul" whenever one of you accidentally or purposefully breaks one of them. You may even choose to agree on a financial fine for each violation!

5

Principles of Wise Parenting

Medical, psychological, and sociological findings about the influence of a child's developmental years on his or her later behavior and attitudes as an adult have brought about renewed interest in what makes a good parent. Recognizing that their children are a precious heritage from God makes most parents eager to raise them "perfectly," which often means improving on their own childhood experience. There is an abiding sense of urgency that has left myriads of modern parents hungry for any morsel of information that will help them do a better job.

The fact that children represent the future of our society and of the church is all the more reason they should be nourished with a careful blend of love and respect. Their feelings must be protected, but they need to be consistently and firmly taught the wisdom of the Lord. Parents who practice the two essential ingredients of raising children—gentle love and sound discipline—are well

81

on their way to developing happy, well-adjusted kids who have appropriate self-esteem. Wise parenting can also reduce the chance of social and emotional problems cropping up later, since many psychological conflicts in adults are traceable to unpleasant childhood experiences.

This section deals with questions on successful child-rearing. Don't expect canned formulas here, since good parenting comes in many flavors. Look instead for useful biblical principles that you can weave into your own Spirit-guided approach to nurturing your children.

My daughter, now thirty, is very shy and emotionally detached. She has battled alcoholism and drug addiction for several years. Shortly after she was born, she had an illness that kept her hospitalized for a month. Could this have affected the bonding between us enough to have caused her present problems?

According to current research, lack of stimulation in infancy dramatically affects a child's developmental pattern. The amount of hugs that babies receive in their first six months has a significant impact on their ability to relate to other people later in life.

Breast-feeding is an ideal opportunity for both physical/emotional bonding between mother and child and stimulation of the infant's physiological systems. Not only does the baby receive helpful antibodies from its mother's milk, but nursing releases a natural hormone in the mother that keeps her serotonin, norepinephrine, and dopamine levels normal. This bodily function diminishes the possibility of postpartum anxiety and depression. Meanwhile, the baby is receiving the kind of attention necessary to set childrearing on a successful path. This is not to say that bottle-fed babies start on a road of failure, but breast-feeding has several unparalleled advantages.

It is indeed possible that your daughter's hospitalization as a newborn did deprive her of needed physical contact and thus may have some correlation with her present emotional detachment. Today, when a young baby must remain in the hospital for postnatal care, the nurses and mother usually give critical physical attention to that baby for a certain period of time every day—sometimes up to two or three hours. Studies have shown that this type of contact is actually as important to a baby as food.

However, it is also very possible that you lavished enough attention on your baby daughter when she came home that you compensated for any earlier deficiency. In spite of your daughter's illness as an infant, she can still overcome her introversion. In fact, this is relatively easy to handle through therapy. A good Christian psychologist or psychiatrist can teach her simple techniques for becoming less detached from others, and can help her overcome any negative effects of that long-ago illness— which, by the way, in *not* your fault!

Group counseling might be especially beneficial in your daughter's case, and this need not be done in a psychologist's office. It can be accomplished through a mini-church or Bible study group where members air their deepest feelings, flaws, and personal prayer requests. You might encourage her to get involved in a church fellowship group where she can share her feelings with others. The shared prayers and the interaction with others may well start her on the road to recovery. For her drug and alcohol problems, she, of course, will need to get professional Christian therapy.

My six-year-old son has a lot of fears. Lately he has been waking up often at night and is afraid to be alone. How can we best handle his fearfulness?

A certain degree of nighttime fear is normal for a six-year-old. Sometimes just providing a night light eases a young child's anxiety. If your son's fearfulness is extreme and continues for more than a few weeks, you might want to ask the opinion of a pediatrician or a child psychiatrist. When your son awakens and calls for you, waiting and watching for a little while at his bedside is advisable. Reassure him and let him talk about what might be upsetting him or causing anxiety in his life. Don't overreact or minimize his concerns if he shares his "deep dark secrets" with you. Your son's feelings are very real to him, and he needs your understanding. Show him how trustworthy you are of his secrets.

Children at your son's age are often uneasy about being separated from Mom and Dad at night. If he gets out of bed and wants to stay with you, calmly lead him back to his room. But do this with a lot of reassurance and comfort, and be sure to stay with him for a while. At first, you might have to sit with him for as long as an hour when he goes to bed, showing your love in a common-sense way. Be sure to consider whether some recent stress at home may be causing him concern—a new baby, family illness, or marital discord.

Our son will not stop biting his nails, and before he started that he sucked his thumb. He is seven years old and has been biting his nails for two years. We are concerned about this habit. How should it be handled?

Although thumb sucking and nail biting are not that unusual, any habit in a child taken to an extreme can indicate underlying anxiety that needs to be dealt with. Overreaction to family pressure can usually be eased through behavior techniques and reassurance. A child psychologist can help you with that. On a deeper level, in-depth counseling may be necessary to discover and work out any hidden problems that are causing excessively anxious behavior. (See the previous question for examples of stress-provoking family situations.)

About 20 percent of children still suck their thumbs after their sixth birthday. However, when a child reaches first grade and still relies on his thumb for comfort, it is usually a sign that family counseling is advisable. Don't worry about moderate nail biting—about 20 percent of *college students* still bite their nails, especially during period of stress.

My husband and I are involved with a Christian pregnancy center and adoption agency. We ask foster families caring for newborns to bond to the infant so the child will have a good chance of making a successful transition into another temporary or permanent home. What advice do you have for the foster family that is left with empty hearts and empty arms over and over again?

Psychiatric research has shown that the first six months of life are very important for teaching a child to trust others. Babies need to be changed when wet, fed when hungry, and hugged when lonely. Psychiatrists regularly see the devastating effects of "malnurturing." A positive experience in infancy is crucial for normal and healthy development later in the child's life, so you are certainly correct in encouraging a foster family to bond strongly with the babies they care for in their homes.

It is inevitable that conscientious foster parents will become truly attached to the newborns they serve. Often, just when they come to love the child, it is time for the baby to leave. Theirs is a tremendous, wonderful ministry. Nothing can diminish the sense of loss that foster parents feel when an infant leaves their home, even when they anticipated this happening. But these rare, remarkable servants can take heart knowing that when the babies are older, trusting God and other people will be easier for them. Gentle nurturing in early infancy launches a child on waves of love.

The best therapy for foster parents is to accept as "normal" the grief they feel at saying "Goodbye." This is a painful loss, and it must involve the five stages of grief discussed in chapter 2. Initial denial that the baby is gone is a natural expression of the loss foster parents feel. But further contact with the child is unwise; the new family needs the freedom to start afresh, apart from the past.

Foster parents must write "The End" to this chapter and accept the reality that the loss is permanent.

In due course of time, the other stages of grief will come and go. Tears may be shed, but encouragement will rise again if foster parents see their role as a ministry. If their service is unto the Lord, foster parents can recognize his plan for the child as taking preeminence. Old hands at foster parenting know that saying "Goodbye" is one of their occupational hazards although they rarely look on their caregiving as a "job." New hands will learn it soon enough. Let them grieve and grow and encourage them to transfer their love to other babies who need what they can provide.

My fifteen-year-old son is very shy. He claims he cannot make friends because he thinks nobody likes him. If I say anything to him about it, he gets irritated. He is a good student, but isn't sports-minded and is generally passive. What can we do to help our son?

There are several things you can do to help your son be more outgoing. First, if his lack of interest in sports is because he is physically weak, encourage him to begin a healthy exercise program. Dad can make a difference here, especially if he does the exercises, too. For example, doing some weightlifting together would not only make your son stronger physically, it would also boost his self-confidence and enhance the father-son relationship. Of course, your son must be given the freedom to make his own decision regarding an exercise program.

Given his shyness, your son may have difficulty joining in with a group, but he probably has one special buddy. Encourage him to bring that friend on family outings. Try planning a weekend camping trip for them. You could even invite the friend's parents to come along. By taking a *gentle* lead in social situations, you remove the pressure from your son to give a sterling performance and make it easier for him to find success in friendship.

Is your son a Christian? Perhaps you need to review the

gospel with him, emphasizing that Jesus is always a great friend. Share your personal testimony of trusting Christ as your Lord and Savior. Many lonely teenagers welcome the Good News of God's love through Jesus Christ, even if they have heard it before. This newfound zeal for the things of God can give isolated youth something in common. Many who have spent their teen years in seclusion come out of their shells in a church youth group and find caring Christian friends.

One of the major issues an adolescent faces is self-image. Unfortunately, too many parents don't know how to help their teenagers through this stage of development. After growing frustrated with constant miscommunication, some parents slip into neutral. Meanwhile, their offspring suffer silently.

Teenagers need love. They still need touching and time spent one-on-one with their parents. Take time to talk, laugh, and have a good time together. Don't try to preach to or think for your son, but rather model healthy adult attitudes and behavior. These meetings can help you stay in close contact with him at this difficult age. He will gradually look forward to sharing his feelings with you and having your undivided attention at certain times. Your sensitivity to his need for affection will keep him aware of the relationship you share, and can possibly help forestall some of the rebellion that often comes with a teenager's search for self-esteem and independence. Be sure to affirm the positive qualities and talents that make your son "special" and unique.

As far as sports are concerned, not everybody finds satisfaction in traditional competition. Maybe your son is better suited for a sport geared to individual skill, such as golf, karate, racquetball, or running. These sports require high levels of personal discipline and also inculcate principles of proper self-confidence. Remember, though, that not everyone is athletically inclined. Encourage physical fitness, but resist the tendency to pressure him in this or any other area.

Finally, consider that a minister to youth, a relative, or some other appropriate mentor may be able to reach your son in ways you cannot. Ask such people to try to establish a relationship with him. Perhaps they will see this as an excellent opportunity for ministry and will be eager to help.

Because of a learning disability, my twins were held back in third grade and also in Sunday school. This has hurt their self-esteem. They want to move up with their friends in Sunday school. It's difficult for them when others keep putting them down. What can I do to help my sons?

If your twins are already unhappy about being held back, their disappointment is bound to continue. (When children reach junior high and high school, they especially want to stay with young people their own age.) Your sons may need another year to catch up academically, but this should not be a concern in Sunday school, where spiritual-emotional maturity is the issue. It would be better for them to stay with their own age group at church, and you should speak to the Sunday school superintendent and ask that this be done. Explain why you believe moving your sons with their age group serves their best interest. If the superintendent does not agree with you, it may be necessary to ask your pastor to intervene. Whatever the outcome, encourage your kids to do the best they can in whatever class they are in. On the other hand, you may need to look for another church, realizing that this might be even more unsettling for your sons.

We have experienced a similar situation in the Meier family. One of my sons had a learning disability in the area of spelling, but he got A's in math and other subjects. I found ways to point out to him the biblical wisdom that we are all designed with certain strengths and weaknesses, and that God does this with a purpose in mind—that each person might uniquely glorify him. I would tell him, "Son, you know how I easily lose my way, especially when I'm thinking about other things. I'm weak in my sense of direction, but there are other areas in which I'm really good. You, too, are really talented in certain areas, Son; you just have some problems with spelling. That's nothing to feel bad about. If you get embarrassed about it at school, remind yourself that God made you with certain talents you can use for him now and even more when you grow up."

My son seems to have accepted that approach very well. It lifted his spirits and renewed his self-esteem, especially when I praised him for the things he does well. For example, he *is* good at sports, so we played a lot of sports together when he was growing up.

You get the idea, I hope. I would encourage you to explain to your sons that everyone on earth has a "learning disability" of some kind, just as everyone has at least one special talent. Help them recognize their strengths, even as you make certain they are getting all the academic help they need. As God works within them, they may one day be able to say with Paul, "When I am weak, then I am strong" (2 Cor. 12:10).

My oldest son is nine and has a moderate case of Tourette's syndrome. He takes 1.5 milligrams of Haldol daily for the body tics he suffers. Naturally, his immaturity causes him to overreact emotionally, and now discipline is a real problem. Would a Christian counselor take a different approach to my son's treatment than his present secular counselor?

Try to find a Christian *child psychiatrist* for him, because he does need the medical treatment. (Incidentally, Haldol *is* an effective drug for Tourette's syndrome.) In addition to the medical care, he will certainly need some counseling. When coupled with proper medical help, counseling will give him the best opportunity to live his life to the fullest. However, there is enough difference between secular and Christian counseling to warrant a switch to a Christian counselor. When your son asks life's tough questions, you will want his therapist to give him biblical rather than humanistic answers.

Our daughter seems afraid of school and often "plays sick" to avoid going. Sometimes after we drop her off at school she runs after our car, crying. We have tried to help her, but have no idea why she is so afraid. When we transferred her to a private school, she coped fine for a few months. But recently she started acting up again. What can we do to solve this problem?

School phobias are not uncommon, and some may reflect an unhealthy basic dependency of a child on a parent, usually the mother. When this problem extends beyond what common-sense solutions will cure, professional counseling may be necessary for not only the child but one or both parents as well. Sometimes what is known in scientific terms as "symbiosis" magnifies the problem. When used in the context of family life, this is a relationship in which parent and child seem to thrive on mutual overdependency. When *any* dependence is extreme, the result can be threatening to either person's mental well-being—or both.

If your daughter is afraid to go to school because she can't bear to be away from home all day, she may indeed be overly dependent on you. Some mothers never allow their children to exercise much independence before entering school. Quite often this happens with the youngest in a large family, which adds to a mother's temptation to spoil the child and resist letting "the baby" grow up. Such children can become quite manipulative, especially if their parents usually let them have their own way and have given them very little discipline.

There are, of course, other reasons that may underlie a child's reluctance to go off to school each day. Even a fairly independent child may be troubled by specific situations at home or school and become anxious in general. For example, school may have become an unpleasant experience because of an overly harsh teacher (at least in the eyes of the child), a classroom bully, or a learning disability that has made it difficult for the child to keep up with the work. Or the child may be excessively shy because of temperament or preschool traumas. Even temporary home stress—a family tragedy, a new baby, or parental disagreements—may be contributing factors. It is important that you check out all these possibilities before deciding that your daughter is just being difficult and needs more discipline. Her "feigned" illnesses may even have some basis in fact, so be sure that she has regular medical checkups.

After ruling out the above factors, including scheduling a conference with your daughter's teachers and comparing notes with her classmates' parents, you may have to exert some "tough love." The best start is to make your daughter understand that she is expected to attend school each day and will not be allowed to stay home under any circumstances. (Of course, you will not force her to attend when there are significant signs of real illness.)

And Mom should not go to school to keep an eye on her, as many are tempted to do. If your daughter runs away from school and comes home, discipline her and take her back immediately. You may need to repeat this a number of times before the child's stubbornness disappears. Strong wills must sometimes be broken or properly channeled, but a child's spirit must remain healthy, so *discipline fairly and with love.*

Both you and your husband must talk together and reevaluate your roles as parents, deciding what they can do to love and discipline their child more effectively. You must both work toward making your child more independent. This is the healthiest path to self-respect, and one that prepares her for life in the real world.

Even in the Christian community there are reports of incest. What exactly is incest, and what are some of its emotional effects on a child?

As the term is commonly used today, "incest" is sexual abuse of a child by a relative—a parent, aunt, uncle, grandparent, or older sibling. Psychologists see thousands of such cases, including incest between mothers and their sons, and fathers with their daughters. A poll taken a few years ago revealed that about 5 percent of adult women and 2 percent of adult men had sexual experiences with a parent or stepparent of the opposite sex while growing up. Those percentages may seem "low." But for something as terrible as incest, the numbers are much too high. Fortunately, while the effects are devastating, most victims are able to eventually lead normal lives, even though they will probably always bear some scars, even if they get good professional Christian therapy.

What you've heard is correct: incest occurs even in the Christian community. Jeremiah was not exaggerating when he quoted the Lord: "The heart is more deceitful than all else. And is desperately sick. Who can understand it?" (Jer. 17:9 NASB). One of our staff members even dealt with a case in which a missionary was committing incest with his daughter, and was using a Scripture verse out of context to justify it.

Consider this case history, and you will better understand the horror of incest. A community leader and his wife appeared to be a model couple, yet they both had sexually abused their daughter since she was about eleven. Her fear was so great throughout childhood that she was never able to tell anyone what she was suffering. She experienced severe emotional pain because of the abuse but was able to find some personal escape through playing the violin. Somehow she managed to do well in school and in time became an accomplished violinist, although she was miserable inside and trusted no one.

In late adolescence, the girl decided to put a stop to the abuse. Because she fought back and refused to allow her parents to have sex with her, they assaulted her, causing permanent damage to a nerve in her right arm. She can no longer play the violin—a critical foundation of her self-esteem and one of the few pleasures she had.

Finally, this young women ran away and moved in with her pastor and his wife, who brought her to a Minirth-Meier hospital program for therapy. She responded well to six weeks of intensive treatment and has learned through the supernatural power of God to forgive her parents, even though they hardly deserve it. This is an actual case study, and it could be retold thousands of times, with minor variations.

Incest victims sometimes feel intense guilt, although they are innocent of wrongdoing. Usually female children are the victims, although we also see men who tell us of long-ago sexual abuse by their mothers. More commonly, incest involves a father and daughter or stepdaughter.

Children crave the love of their parents. If a child does not receive the proper kind of affection and has not experienced a healthy family relationship, he or she may eventually succumb to incestuous advances as a means of receiving much wanted attention. If the incest begins at an early age, which it often does, the child has no concept of what is happening, much less that it is wrong.

Dads sometimes treat their daughters as "girl friends," acting carelessly seductive with them, especially if they are otherwise unhappy. Never mistake this kind of behavior as love! Love never seeks to hurt and destroy, and love does not rejoice in iniquity. Certainly God forgives even this terrible sin, and Jesus died on the cross to redeem *all* sinners. But we must recognize exactly how horrible that sin is and just how disturbed the perpetrators are.

A father may begin abusing his daughter when she reaches early adolescence and starts looking like a woman. A common line incestuous fathers use is, "This is my way of showing that I love you." It is incredible, but many girls will believe their fathers because, as a rule, children *want* to believe what their parents say. Some girls may even be willing participants at first. Even if they are unwilling and realize that what is happening is wrong, fear of a parent's wrath and a normal tendency to submit to that parent's authority keep them unwilling to resist or complain.

Typically, the father will use "blackmail," as in "Keep this a secret, or else I'll go to jail, and our whole family will be destroyed. Terrible things are going to happen if you tell." Or he may be more subtle, playing on his daughter's sympathy by telling her how unhappy he is with his job, her mother, or life in general—and that only she understands him. By whatever means, he enlists the girl in a conspiracy of silence, although, ironically, the mother usually at least suspects what is going on but does not risk intervening, for a variety of reasons.

Guilt feelings will intensify in later years, as the girl finally figures out that the incestuous acts were wrong. These feelings may make her ashamed to tell her mother or anyone else. Mothers are often passive participants, sometimes because they sleep in a different bedroom and ignore the father's sexual needs, or because they have been physically abused by their husband or as a young child were abused by their father. A mother who allows her daughter to be sexually abused by her father is just as guilty as he is. When parents are confronted with the suspicion of incest, they almost always deny it. Yet, it is very rare for children to fabricate such a story.

Anger is another common aftermath of incest. When a daughter realizes the truth—that Dad has been using her and doesn't really love her—she develops tremendous bitterness toward him. There may be a happy ending—she meets a nice man later and marries him—but usually this doesn't happen. Instead, she will develop crushes on sociopathic men, repeating the unhealthy behavior pattern of childhood. And, unfortunately, in too many cases the pattern of abuse is passed along to her children.

Incest victims can have great difficulty enjoying a physical relationship in marriage as a result of psychological blocks from their early years. Bad memories of the abuse they suffered actually prevents the chemical and neurological releases that enable a person to enjoy sexual intimacy. With therapy, however, most incest victims can recover totally.

Some incest victims falsely blame themselves, so they develop extremely low self-esteem and become self-abusive or suicidally depressed. Sometimes they mutilate themselves or do other self-destructive things to enact personal punishment. Others seek ways to fail in life and continue hurting themselves because they are really angry at their parents but believe it is sinful to show anything but "honor" toward a mother or father. Incest victims must learn that it's okay to be angry, but they need to recognize just exactly who was the guilty one and forgive that person, if only for the sake of starting the healing process. The law requires that the incestuous parent must be turned in to the proper authorities to protect future potential victims.

With Christian inpatient or outpatient counseling, incest victims start becoming aware of the rage they have stored inside and the ways to express it. Prayer and careful guidance will help them overcome the anger and learn how to forgive the person who has violated them. Then comes the supernatural healing. Incest victims need to turnover to God any feelings of vengeance before they can begin again with their lives. The victim needs to be reminded that unless the abuser genuinely repents, God will severely punish such sin.

When we were grade-school age, my sister and I were sexually abused by a close and trusted family relative. No one even suspected. Somehow I mentally blocked it out for a few years. One day during my high school years I came home to find my sister and mother crying. When my mother asked me about the abuse, the memories all came rushing back. Since then I've had nightmares and still have problems relating intimately to my husband. I'm afraid something similar might happen to my children, but I'm also afraid of being overprotective. Fortunately, I

became a Christian in college, but my sister later commit-
ted suicide. I think it was because she never received any
help. Is there a "cure" for those who suffer the hurt of
incest?

Dealing with incest is a long process that must begin
with some very simple and clear steps on behalf of the
victim:

1. Remove the victim from the molester's immediate
   environment (or vice versa).
2. Call a social agency or police department and
   report what has happened.
3. Introduce the victim into personal Christian counseling to deal with the emotional hurt and bitterness.
4. Work toward having the victim or a responsible
   adult confront the molester.
5. Take preventive measures to stop recurrences.

Many people are naive about the rise of incest in our
society. Perhaps you *are* a somewhat "overprotective"
mother, but it is better to be careful than blindly trusting.
Choose babysitters wisely, using only trusted caregivers.
Later, have a casual conversation with your children to be
sure they were treated fairly and properly by the baby-
sitter. Don't say anything that might alarm the children.
Just ask simple questions in a casual fashion. (There are
many helpful booklets now available that explain how a
parent can best educate a child about sexual molestation,
even at an early age.)

An incest victim must be protected from further
molestation, even if the guilty party is one of the child's
parents. In one particularly shocking case, a father
impregnated his thirteen-year-old daughter and later
impregnated his teenaged granddaughter. How could this
happen? No one stopped him.

If outside intervention becomes necessary, someone
needs to call the authorities and report the molester. Social

agencies can help, especially a local child-welfare organization. An agency representative or law-enforcement officer will have a conversation with the molester and put him (or her) on the alert that his behavior is being monitored. This is an important step in helping the victim and safeguarding other potential victims. If the molestation has been long-term and habitual, criminal charges will most likely be filed. Sexual abusers who are not stopped will almost certainly repeat their criminal behavior. Even if they are not prosecuted, they will need counseling.

As for your own situation, you need the benefit of personal counseling. A Christian counselor who knows how to practice insight-oriented therapy can help you uncover and settle old grudges. If you don't deal with the inner hurt, you will continue to be victimized long after the fact. Serious depression might result. As you progress in counseling and your conflicts are resolved, your marriage will improve, both physically and emotionally. If you have not already done so, share your feelings about the long-ago incidents with your husband. Many victims of childhood sexual abuse have difficulty trusting members of the opposite sex enough to achieve a fulfilling marital relationship without in-depth therapy.

Counseling should continue until you can sleep in peace without having nightmares. This will mark the beginning of real progress. Soon after this you should be able to fully enjoy your relationship with your husband and live a totally normal and healthy life. You are an innocent victim, and God wants to rid you of the heavy weight you have been carrying for so long.

Sometimes it is worthwhile for incest victims to eventually confront the person who molested them. This can be healthy for several reasons. One is that the Bible says to do so, in both Leviticus 19 and elsewhere, including the New Testament. Airing your grievance makes you face your emotions, may help the offender, and serves as a warning that could deter him from hurting others in the future. Confrontation can begin a chain reaction of positive effects.

If you don't want a face-to-face encounter, phone or write the relative who abused you and let him know that you haven't forgotten what he did to you and your sister. If too much time has passed for reporting the crime, tell him you have chosen to forgive him. Then let God punish him in any way he sees fit. Encourage the man to repent and seek counseling—but expect him to lie to you. When confronted with sexual sins, the guilty often act repentant, but not always. Some even deny the acts ever occurred. Consider contacting your molester's wife and other family members so that other children are safeguarded from his advances.

After a confrontation, have no further contact with this person. Protect yourself and your family. Guard your emotional stability, and thank God for enabling you to face the person who brought you the greatest pain you have ever known.

Know, too, that God holds that man accountable for damaging your sister so severely that it eventually led to her death. Her rage toward her abuser was so great that she turned the anger on herself and killed herself out of an overwhelming sense of *false* guilt. A young person's total self-concept is often ruined by incest that occurred years before. Many victims become sexually promiscuous in an unending search for approval and "love," as defined by their molester. Others survive the best they can as they try to bury their pain. Unfortunately, some choose the path your sister did.

The memories of incest can be healed, but the sensitivity of the scars can take some time to wear away. In most cases professional counseling is required to uncover the long-buried emotions. Hospitalization in a Christian psychiatric unit may be necessary if the victim cannot function adequately or is feeling suicidal.

When I was a nine-year-old girl, I sexually molested my two-year-old niece. Now she is twenty, and I'm almost thirty. I really struggle with what I did, even though it happened only a couple of times. Still, the guilt nags at me. I've asked for God's forgiveness but sometimes don't feel forgiven. I wonder, "Why would I abuse a small child when I was young?" I love children and would never want to hurt anyone. How can I deal with this guilt?

Children from the ages of nine to eleven are naturally curious about sexual matters. This is true for boys and girls alike. "Experimentation" is the rule rather than the exception. Many children have done what you did—satisfying their curiosity by discovering facts about the human body, their own and another child's.

You should not feel guilty for what you did when you were nine. You have confessed it to the Lord and asked him to forgive you. He has promised that if we sincerely repent and ask for forgiveness, he removes our sins as far as the east is from the west and buries them in the deepest sea. "Though your sins are like scarlet, they shall be as white as snow" (Isa. 1:18). You are forgiven by God, but since you are obviously a very conscientious person, guilt is still haunting you about this many years later.

Since your niece was only two when the two incidents happened, she probably does not remember them. Do not bring up the matter with her unless you believe she remembers something, especially if she asks you about it. There is no need to stir up negative feelings over something that may be long forgotten. If she should say something to you about it, you might say, "I remember doing that when I was young, and for many years I have wanted to ask your forgiveness." Again, though, it is highly unlikely that she will ever remember much of anything that happened when she was two years old.

More importantly, you need to learn to forgive yourself. If your self-punishing struggle lingers much longer, perhaps you should seek counseling. Satan often uses false or exaggerated guilt to prevent us from being effective for the Lord. He is haunting your perfectionistic nature with old memories, effectively getting you to hold grudges against yourself. The inner disappointment you feel toward yourself is way out of proportion to what you did as a child to satisfy your immature curiosity. Inability to forgive ourselves reflects a subconscious unwillingness to trust God's promise of redemption.

It is a sin to hold grudges against yourself when the sin is already confessed. You have a secret desire to enact revenge on yourself, but even that kind of vengeance is not *your* prerogative. All vengeance is God's alone. But God doesn't want to punish you; he forgave you the first time you asked in sincere repentance. Don't reject this great truth, which is the heart of the gospel message. Rather, accept it and thank God for his grace.

It is unlikely you would ever commit this kind of act as an adult. You are obviously a good person, not at all a "child molester." There is a difference between sexual abuse and childhood experimentation, and it is very important to recognize the difference.

I recently discovered that my husband sexually molested his sisters when he was a teenager. He swears that he has never done anything like that to our daughter, but where do I draw the line between forgiveness and trusting him while protecting my daughter?

Although your husband may be telling you the truth, it is not wise to trust him totally. Look at this matter realistically. The older he was when he abused his sisters, the greater the possibility it could happen again. Of course, this doesn't mean it will happen, only that it could.

If your husband was merely a curious adolescent at the time of the incidents, the abusive behavior could be quickly forgiven and dismissed. That is not to diminish the sinfulness of adolescent molestation, but simply to say that such behavior does not necessarily have a far-reaching impact on how the abuser will act later on.

What should you do under the circumstances? First,

talk to your daughter about sexual abuse in general. Tell her that although most men and women respect and love little children, there are others who do unkind things. Don't put down all men, or make it sound as if no man can be trusted. Gently warn her about what molestation is and make it easy for her to report any unusual touching to you. Boys need to be warned as well.

Children should be instructed to tell their parents if *anyone* ever fondles or touches their bodies in a way that makes them uneasy. Let them know that such behavior should not be allowed and should never be kept secret from Mom and Dad—no matter what the other person says and who the other person is. With loving instructions like these, a molested child will be less fearful of telling. In fact, have your child *promise* to tell you if anyone so much as tries to touch her private area, because prevention is the best step in curing this increasing problem. Accept your husband's promise never to repeat his molesting behavior with your daughter (or anyone else), but maintain a watchful attitude. Confront him if anything about your daughter's behavior or conversation arouses your suspicion that he has made sexual overtures toward her.

My six-year-old daughter is showing a real need to be independent. Sometimes she plainly defies me. When I ask her to do something, she might say "No!" or see if she can get away with speaking to me in a disrespectful tone of voice. How can I relate to her without using imperatives and allow her to feel free to make her own decisions in appropriate areas?

"Imperative" thinking, which involves "shoulds" and "shouldn'ts," is best avoided in adult-to-adult communication. It does have a place, however, in adult-to-child relationships.

Although we need to accept children unconditionally and want to teach them to think for themselves, there is a necessary behavioral structure that can be created for them through the careful practice of biblical guidelines and standards. They need this for security. They need to know that when Mom says, "I want you to pick up your toys and have it done in three minutes," it is an imperative that will carry some unpleasant consequences if not obeyed. The adult-to-child relationship needs to be more rule-oriented and structured than an adult-to-adult relationship. Be sure you can distinguish between the two, and then use appropriate communicating.

As long as your rules and expectations are realistic, don't worry about being overly imperative with your daughter. She needs to learn how to respond to authority figures; this is an important part of the real world. The younger she learns this, the better it will be for her later in life when she is on her own, yet still subject to society's rules.

On an adult-to-adult level, however, it is right to avoid imposing imperatives on others. On occasion this is necessary, such as in an employer-employee relationship. Among friends and other adult associates and relatives, we must recognize others' autonomy. Using imperatives with our peers tends to drive them away, and any hope for a ministry to them (or even a friendship) is lost.

We've been having problems with our seventeen-year-old daughter, and now she has run away from home. She has turned to a friend, who has taken her in. We worry that the sympathy she's receiving is dulling her better judgment. Our daughter is bright, but has always complained that we are "too strict." What can we do about this situation?

First, you must begin loving your daughter unconditionally. By a telephone or note, let her know that you love her no matter what she does, that you love her even though she has run away but want to understand what is bothering her. Explain that you know she disagrees with your rules, but that this changes neither your love for her nor your belief that some rules are necessary for her well-being. If you remain calm and nonjudgmental, you can probably get your daughter to meet with you for a *two-way* conversation about your differences.

Once your daughter agrees to a meeting, also encourage her to visit a Christian counselor with you, "just to see what he or she says." Explain that you're willing to learn what you may be doing wrong. This means admitting that you've made mistakes, too. Settling matters with your daughter at this time is very important, because she will be out on her own in another year or two. A Christian counselor who is trained in family therapy will under-stand the family dynamics by listening to you both and will help you formulate a specific plan of action.

If your daughter returns home on a trial basis, one good technique is to make written family contracts. This allows the whole family to negotiate together and decide on some house rules and the consequences of certain "violations." All family members will have a vote, but they also must listen to each other and to what the coun-selor recommends. A written contract with a teenager usually works well in correcting rebellious behavior and provides a workable structure at home.

If your daughter refuses to meet with you or come home, all you can do is to keep loving and praying for her. Try to stay in contact with her and let her know that she is always welcome to return provided she agrees to abide by the terms of the contract you have worked out together. You might request, "If you decide to stay away, please call at least once a week so we'll know you're okay." This will give you a weekly opportunity to remind her that you still love her and will make a reconciliation more probable.

I've been told that I have a strong, obsessive-compulsive personality. Perhaps that is true, because I know I am a perfectionist and have high standards that my spouse calls "unreasonable." I felt hurt by similar negative traits in my own parents. How can I avoid damaging my daughter by my excessive demands yet maintain the discipline any child needs?

One way to relax some "unreasonable" standards is to have more kids as quickly as possible! That sounds like peculiar advice, but if you have several children, you will be too worn out to be a perfectionist with them.

Perfectionists really do a better job as parents if they have more than one child. Most parents tend to put too many expectations on the first child anyway, which is rather unfair. That's one reason why being an only child can be tough. Many only children feel appropriately sorry for themselves for having been the one in whom all their parents' hopes and dreams were invested.

Chat with some successful parents in your church who have raised three or four children. Ask them what their rules were and what they think about areas of child-rearing you have questions about. Even if you don't agree with their approach, it helps to have feedback.

Look carefully at your expectations and rules. Are some of them unnecessary or unreasonable? Try to see your strict parenting techniques from your daughter's perspective. Remember that she is already her own person and has the right to think, feel, and desire for herself. Don't overstep your boundaries as a parent by attempting to control things beyond your "jurisdiction." Let her express her feelings about the standards you have set, and then work together on a compromise.

It often helps to allow children to have some input into parenting and discipline techniques. Any loving family can sit down and write out one or more family contracts, outlining specific behaviors, expectations, rules, and appropriate consequences for violations that everyone agrees on. Even young children appreciate this alternative to hard-line discipline. Everyone gets a vote on family contracts even though the parents maintain ultimate veto power.

I was a full-time nurse before we had our first baby. I stopped working to take care of her, but I recently started a job in the evening. My husband takes care of our little girl during that time, but I feel guilty about leaving her, even though I'm gone for only a few hours. My husband says it does me good to get out of the house. I feel strongly that a mother should be with her child most of the time. Could my absence have a detrimental effect on our child?

We certainly encourage mothers to be at home with their children, but a few hours away several nights each week probably will not harm your child. This will give your husband time with your daughter, so that he can bond with her, too. It is only extended or frequent absence that causes problems for a young child. If a mother is gone often, especially if the baby is left with someone who is not warm and caring, normal development could be hindered. Your particular situation, however, seems reasonable.

A factor you should look at carefully, however, is whether being away from your husband during the days when he works and again during the evenings when you work might harm your marital relationship. A better schedule might be for him to work less so you can spend more time together or to limit your work to from one to three nights a week.

My eight-year-old son seems overly energetic and has difficulty concentrating on schoolwork. A friend recently told me about "attention-deficit disorder." Is it possible my son has this problem, and, if so, what can I do about it?

Attention-deficit disorder (ADD) is a very complex syndrome. In the past it was called Minimal Brain Dysfunction. Because diagnosing ADD is not a simple matter, this analysis should be done only by a child psychiatrist who has training and experience with the disorder.

Usually, a cluster of symptoms characterizes ADD.

These may include neurological symptoms as well as shortened attention span, inability to concentrate, hyperactivity (in some cases), and some acting-out types of behavior. Diagnosis should be made carefully to rule out any underlying neurological or other medical causes for the abnormal behavior. This disorder can also be associated with certain learning disabilities. Generally, ADD is a childhood disorder, affecting children (more commonly boys) between the ages of five and twelve, but in rare instances it appears in adults.

Treatment for ADD is a controversial issue. Two of the most commonly prescribed medications include Ritalin and Cylert. These drugs may work by heightening the nervous system's ability to screen incoming stimuli, allowing the child to focus attention on one area of interest at a time. The child can then maintain a higher level of concentration and a lengthened attention span.

It is theorized that these medications correct a possible dopamine imbalance in the brain, but medical science has no conclusive proof of this. Without medication, ADD interrupts the learning process, social development is hindered, and behavior problems usually worsen, especially at school. These factors frequently are sufficient cause to begin using medication on a trial basis. The controversy surrounding these medications arises because both are amphetamines and can be mildly addicting, but usually very low doses are prescribed.

The prognosis for an ADD patient is very good if medication is used properly. These drugs should be used only for actual cases of ADD, not just for anxiety and other emotional disturbances or for nonrelated learning disabilities. When treating ADD with Ritalin or Cylert, the benefits must be weighed against the risks: the slight chance of stunted growth and/or addiction. Naturally, such medications should be carefully monitored during the course of treatment. Cautious observation of the child by the doctor, parents, and teachers will reveal whether normal growth is being affected, or if overdependence on the medication is developing. If signs of either slow growth or addiction occur, steps should be taken to correct the problem. After a brief period of discontinued use, undesirable symptoms can be reversed.

To be thoroughly effective, treatment of ADD with medication must be coupled with counseling by a qualified professional. Properly administered medication and regular therapy work with most ADD children. It is possible for the symptoms to be eliminated and the children to go on to normal lives and even above-average accomplishments.

When ADD children are reluctant to take long-term medication, effective treatment breaks down. Although they behave and concentrate much better with medication, they sometimes claim they don't feel "normal" because of their ongoing need for the drugs. It helps to involve these children in the decision to take medication. Otherwise, they may become only irregular participants in the treatment process, which will be detrimental to progress and eventual recovery.

A vacation from the medication can be given every six months to give you and the physician an opportunity to see if the symptoms of ADD are lessening spontaneously. If they are, the medication can be safely discontinued, and the child usually lives a normal life without further treatment.

Children with ADD are typically bright, with average or above-average intelligence, but their short attention span and unseemly behavior often cause them to be mislabeled as problem children. It is vital that children with ADD receive treatment to help them overcome their dysfunctioning and start them on the road to normalcy. Many children with ADD outgrow it during adolescence. ADD is rarely treated after the teenage years, because the symptoms commonly diminish over time.

6

Personality-Based Concerns

Your personality is the sum total of all your behavioral traits and patterns, your thoughts, feelings, motives, attitudes, and unconscious dynamics. It is very complex and was formed by your genes, your environmental influences (especially in the first six years of your life), and the choices you have personally chosen to make throughout your life.

Your personality is not locked in cement. With God's help and the help of fellow human beings, you can choose to grow and change, although changing your personality is itself a difficult and complex task. That is why we rely on Jesus Christ as our source of power.

The world of psychotherapy generally recognizes several basic personality types. None of us possesses all the characteristics of a single type, but we are all endowed with a mixture of various traits—tendencies to react emotionally and behaviorally in specific ways. God created each of us "wonderfully and fearfully," which means that

109

we are provided with unique talents and traits. Ironically, our greatest strengths are sometimes our most bothersome liabilities—that is, when they are exaggerated and out of control.

This section presents key problems that accompany a few of the more common personality types. While it is likely that you will relate strongly to *some* of the questions (as in other sections of this book), remember that each of us must deal with our own "personality problems" uniquely. Because there are so many variables, there are no easy formulas, no quick fixes. The suggestions presented in this chapter no doubt will be helpful, but be careful not to equate the difficulties you may be facing with those encountered by someone else. *In certain cases,* understanding the basic concepts and administering these guidelines cannot substitute for proper treatment by a professional.

My obsessive-compulsive personality interferes with my ability to walk with the Lord and relate to others successfully. As a child, I was the object of ridicule by my overdemanding parents. Now I tend to be overly critical of others—though I'm highly critical of myself as well. How can I achieve balance in my life and be free from my fears and compulsions to be "perfect?"

Obsessiveness is the hallmark of the perfectionist and is fueled by the fear of criticism, rejection, and failure. The solution is much easier said than done: Rest in the reality that God loves you and gives you his unconditional acceptance. This insight allows you to accept your own limitations—you have the freedom to fail! Errors are a part of everyone's life. You can fail and not be a failure, or you can fail and become a failure. The choice is yours.

Instead of badgering yourself with self-criticism when mistakes occur, stop to ask God what he wants you to learn from what has happened, and how you can grow because of it. You can do your "best" in striving for a specific goal only once in a lifetime. All other days, you will come a little short of "the best," at least in terms of *that* goal.

If you're really a perfectionist, you are never satisfied with any achievement. You say to yourself, "Tomorrow could be my best—better than my last best." What you are really doing is setting ever-higher goals for yourself, and some of them may be quite unrealistic, usually because one or both of your parents conditionally accepted you and expected too much of you. Give up on pleasing that parent. God is easier to please because he knows you are human.

Lower your day-by-day goals to what you consider "average," and therefore attainable. That grates on you, doesn't it? The idea of "average" is more than you can contemplate as acceptable. Still, if you make this your practice, the reality of reaching your "best" is much more likely. Normal performance for the perfectionist is well above average for most people. The perfectionist's "average" is reachable; the perfectionist's "extraordinary" usually requires superhuman qualities or divine intervention.

Let God love you; then set only attainable goals for yourself. These two exercises alone will enable you to accept the "shortcomings" of others as well, since you will then realize that only by *your* inflated criteria are they shortcomings.

My husband is an obsessive-compulsive, and he works with a woman with a histrionic personality type. She is very dramatic, animated, and has a flair for the unusual. She isn't dependable and is often late. My husband has a hard time working with this woman. Do you have any suggestions on how he can improve their on-the-job relationship?

You *should* be concerned about your husband's workday associates, perhaps in an area you have not yet considered. Obsessive-compulsives often have difficulty expressing their feelings, whereas histrionic personalities are not only "emotional," but often let their feelings get out of control. This can trigger similar reactions, even in obsessive-compulsives. Because histrionics sometimes are attracted to obsessives, your husband needs to be aware of his potential susceptibility and use common sense when alone with this woman.

You can help him best by warning him—gently, of course, and with no implication that you do not trust him. His co-worker might not consciously try to seduce him. A compromising situation may occur simply because her dramatics are misinterpreted. Your husband may mistake her friendly informality as attraction to his charm, looks, or intelligence. The possibility exists that your husband's co-worker may subconsciously want to initiate an affair as an indirect way to remove the pressure of his perfectionistic demands at work. Warning him about the potential dynamics of such a relationship could be important, as could helping him see that he may well be expecting too much in the way of her job performance.

Your husband's co-worker needs help too. She will respond best to honest, straightforward guidelines. For example, if she is continually late and your husband is her supervisor, he could request that she be on time or her salary will be docked. As this woman's supervisor, he should make sure that she clearly understands her job responsibilities. Perhaps he *is* demanding too much of her. However, either of these suggestions is more difficult to implement if they work at the same level, for—in that case—he has no managerial control over her performance. Then he must rely on convincing her that working cooperatively is important for their mutual success in the workplace.

People with extremely emotional personalities need clearly defined limitations. Of course, they also need kindness and acceptance, as we all do. Histrionic personalities are good at demonstrating their feelings but are not always so skilled at thinking through situations. They respond best to specific requests, offered calmly and in kindness. Animated and highly imaginative people can be a terrific asset to any business but must be kept under judicious control. They make good salespersons but are often poor managers. (Histrionic personality patterns are discussed at length later in this chapter.)

I stopped dating five years ago when I became a Christian because I wanted to "wait on the Lord" for the perfect man. I realized recently how totally unrealistic this is and decided to be less judgmental about the men I meet. Four months ago, I met a man who was recently divorced because his wife had been involved in an affair. We began dating each other in what seemed like a good relationship, but he stopped seeing me after two months. I have been diagnosed as being "co-dependent," and his rejection has been very hard to accept. Do you have any suggestions for dealing with my feelings?

Co-dependency is one form of "unhealthy" love (see chapter 4 for further discussion of this). The term can have several applications, but it is often used to refer to a relationship in which one person (or both) is overly dependent on the other as a total source of gratification. Dependency is not unhealthy in itself, since we humans are social beings, and marriage partners, relatives, friends, and co-workers must be able to rely on each other in varying ways and degrees. A "normal" human connection involves mutuality—giving and receiving support and affirmation without submerging the personality of either party.

Dependency can become inappropriate—and love is "addictive"—when we expect someone else to think for us, make our decisions, solve our problems, and satisfy our every whim. It is just as unhealthy to take over all those functions on another's behalf. Some women, for example, fall in love only with a man who is "needy," believing that the more indispensable she becomes to him, the more tightly he will cling to her. If the weak

individual gets well, the perpetual caregiver will no longer
be attracted to him and will probably start looking for
someone else to save. An example of this would be a
woman who marries one alcoholic, then another, so she
will always be needed—just as she was needed to pick up
the pieces for her alcoholic father years before.

Of course, the other side of a co-dependency situation
is that—once healed—the "rescued one" may reject his or
her helper and move on alone. This may or may not be
the case in your situation. The first step in handling your
feelings about this man is deciding whether your severed
relationship had any long-term potential. Perhaps he just
got cold feet about trusting you and making a commitment because he has already been burned once. He may
actually care for you a lot and still be tentative about
putting his emotions on the line. If you believe you have a
chance together, it is worth trying to renew your friendship. But be ready to take "no" for an answer if that's
what you get. You may have to accept that this relationship was not meant to be.

God does not want us to live without the comfort of
intimate relationships. Search for what is worthwhile in
all your person-to-person associations and be ready to dis-
card any that damage your self-esteem. Victims of
unhealthy relationships fail to see themselves from God's
perspective. This takes practice, patience, prayer, and
daily meditation in the Scriptures. You need to see yourself as God sees you. He loves you. In fact, he thinks
you're so wonderful that he sent his only Son to die for
you. Measure the way you think of yourself by the way
God thinks of you. With such a view you can find the
road to many healthy relationships.

*Can you inherit "depression"? And can you outgrow it?
My husband is a manic-depressive, and I wonder if our
children are likely to be manic-depressive as well, or
inherit personalities that have too many ups and downs.*

Most so-called depression is not inherited. Unfortunately, however, if your husband has been diagnosed as "manic-depressive," he has the kind of disorder that is genetically related. About one percent of the population has true manic-depressive illness. Most of these people live normal lives until about the age of twenty. This is when the mood swings begin—times of super highs, others of devastating lows. Bipolar manics may even become suicidally depressed.

Manic-depressives can be helped to lead normal lives through the careful use of medication. Common prescriptions include Mellaril, Navane, and Lithium during the manic phase. Various antidepressants are used during the low state. Some victims need lithium all their lives during all phases.

You might be surprised to know that there are some positive aspects of this condition. Manic-depressives tend to be productive workers and quite energetic when they are experiencing a "high." If the severity of their symptoms is controlled (by medication), some make great salesmen; others run their own companies.

Since only one parent is manic-depressive, your children have less than a 10 percent chance of inheriting this mental disorder. In terms suitable to their age level, you might sensitively and carefully explain what their dad has been going through. Toward mid- to late-adolescence, begin preparing them for any symptoms and related problems they might experience.

If one of them does develop true manic-depression, be sure he or she is under the care of a psychiatrist, preferably one with a Christian orientation. Counseling visits about every three months (perhaps throughout life) often prove effective after the initial consultation. Sound counseling coupled with the wise use of medication will most likely make the joys of a normal life possible.

Therapy enables manic-depressives to get in touch with their anger and extreme volatility. They probably need to find forgiveness in their hearts. Although many textbooks trace the disorder to genetic factors, some room must be left for experiential and spiritual aspects of the problem. Life events significantly influence manic-depressives. That is, frustrations that might make an average person temporarily depressed can cause a manic to become temperamental, moody, or filled with unbridled rage. By learning to become aware of their anger without being embarrassed and to forgive without holding grudges (Rom. 12:14–21; Eph. 4:26; Lev. 19:17–18), manic-depressives can diminish the frequency and severity of their mood swings.

Generally speaking, there is no way to predict at what age manic or depressive episodes will begin, because most affected people live ordinary lives until after adolescence. They suddenly begin to expect too much of themselves and others. Typically, they often insist on working long hours. Or, to soothe the effects of their mood swings, some manic-depressives turn to alcohol. In either case, reality gradually becomes a blur, and there may be hallucinatory experiences.

A housewife, for example, might stay up all night cleaning her house, "talking to angels," or believing she possesses "the key to the universe." A respected businessman might suddenly disrobe and streak down Main Street or go from bar to bar telling people he is the risen Lord. Manic-depressive behavior can be very bizarre and frightening.

After receiving medication for about ten days, these same people often return to normal lives. They usually remember what they have done, and they become understandably embarrassed. They think, "Oh, no! Did I really do that?"

True manic-depressives are innocent victims of a biochemical abnormality. They are ill, but should not be pitied, just loved. And they must be encouraged to handle their affliction through counseling and any medication that is prescribed. A milder variety of bipolar symptoms is found in persons with cyclothymic personalities. Their high periods are "hypomanic" (not quite manic), and they have depressive (but usually not suicidal) mood swings as well. The causes are generally partially genetic and partially due to environmental factors and personal lifelong choices. Long-term Christian outpatient therapy is usually sufficient but sometimes medication may be necessary.

What are some of the symptoms of "clinical depression," and how can I overcome it in a biblical way?

Depression is probably the most painful emotion. Each of us has sometimes felt temporarily depressed, but *clinical depression* is long-lasting and can be identified by five major symptoms:

1. A "sad affect," or sorrowful appearance. In Genesis 4:6–7 we see that Cain had a "downcast" countenance.
2. Painful thinking. Depressed people feel blue, dejected, hopeless, worthless, and believe they will never feel better. Suicide may seem like a realistic solution to a seriously depressed person. Psalms 42 and 43 reveal some key aspects of the painful thinking of depression.
3. Anxiety. Generalized fearfulness and depression typically act together, causing irritability or apathy and feelings of social incompetence.
4. Physical and medical symptoms. Clinically depressed people have difficulty sleeping through the night (or they sleep too much) and may stop eating. They are lethargic, have low energy, and lack motivation. They may have trouble concentrating.
5. Delusional thoughts or voices. These are illusory, of course, but seem very real to the severely depressed person. Only 3 percent of depressed persons develop delusions or hallucinations.

Overcoming depression and anxiety and achieving a wholesome mental balance are more fully discussed in chapters 1 and 2, and thoroughly discussed in our book,

Happiness Is a Choice (Baker, 1978). A brief review here
of some basic guidelines may be helpful:

Daily commit your life to glorifying Jesus Christ.

Meditate on God's Word each day.

Resolve grudges daily, since grudges are the primary
cause of the biochemical changes that result in
depressive symptoms.

Spend time every day with family members.

Spend time each week bonding with Christian friends.

Develop a personally satisfying daily routine.

Do something special for one person at least once a
week to get your mind off yourself part of the time.

**Our adult daughter has been in counseling for several
years and still lives with us. She has been diagnosed as
"borderline mentally ill," but we have never told her
this. I have a three-part question: (1) should she be told;
(2) can medication help; and (3) is it possible she will
ever lead a normal life?**

"Borderline mentally ill" is a broad diagnosis that may
refer to "borderline personality." The latter is a very popular term and is frequently overused. It seems that these
days anybody with generalized emotional problems is
considered "borderline" something.

A *borderline personality* is indicated by several specific
character traits, including mood swings, anger, identity
problems, feelings of loneliness, and co-dependence. *Any*
of these characteristics can be present in true mental illness, but in a much more exaggerated form.

Both you and your daughter's counselor should be honest and up front with her and tell her exactly what the
diagnosis means. Honesty with patients is imperative if
they are expected to be honest in return.

Sometimes medication can help these people cope with
daily living, but it is not quite as helpful here as it is with

other types of marginal disorders. Your daughter's condition probably is curable, and long-term therapy should help her become emotionally mature. She can certainly come to enjoy life to the fullest, especially with your encouragement and assistance in the counseling process. Long-term outpatient therapy for one or more years will probably be required. Brief hospitalizations may also be needed during times of suicidal impulses.

My thirty-eight-year-old brother had an extremely introverted personality growing up but then developed schizophrenia at age eighteen. When he was first diagnosed, my dad wanted to be unconditionally loving but firm, and do what was best. Because my mother considered it rejection to institutionalize my brother, the first ten years of his illness my brother was home most of the time. He eventually became aggressive, probably because he was off his medication. This led my dad to place him under permanent care. Since then, Dad has had a stroke and is now in a nursing home. Mom let my brother come back home, but one morning he took a knife and threatened her life because he didn't want to take his medicine. Sometime after the police arrested him, my brother broke away and jumped off a bridge into a river. He is now in jail. Do you have any insight and advice for us?

Most introverted personalities never develop serious mental disorders like schizophrenia. Introverts are shy people, primarily due to environmental factors such as lack of stimulation in infancy. Many were discouraged from sharing anger and other emotions as young children. Group therapy or church growth groups help them a great deal.

However, because your brother is mentally ill, he is unaware of what he is doing much of the time. He is potentially dangerous, especially since he will not take his medicine. Unfortunately, your sad story is all too common when schizophrenia is the diagnosis.

Schizophrenia is a mental disease that affects about one out of every hundred people. Although schizophrenia is primarily inherited, it may skip one or two generations; it is not inevitable that other family members will develop this illness. If symptoms do not occur before the age of thirty, the likelihood of a later appearance is slim. Schizophrenia usually first occurs in the late teens or early twenties. Many, but not all, schizophrenics were introverted personalities growing up, but many schizophrenics were normal and outgoing prior to their break with reality.

Schizophrenia is correlated with a chemical imbalance in the brain and causes varying degrees of abnormal behavior, ranging from extreme withdrawal to violence. There is a basic loss of touch with reality, and visual and/or (usually) auditory hallucinations may be experienced.

Some people have a mild form of schizophrenia and do quite well. Through the proper use of medication and ongoing counseling, these patients can enjoy marriage, family life, and a productive career.

There is no "cure" for schizophrenia. However, with prompt medical intervention after a patient's first break with reality, it is often possible for ordinary behavior to return. Conversely, once a schizophrenic has battled the disorder for a number of years without treatment, the prognosis is less encouraging. In fact, after being out of touch with reality for over six months, seldom can the symptoms be controlled, even with proper medical treatment. Many schizophrenics can function normally if treated early enough and supervised properly.

In your brother's case, it may be necessary for you to obtain a court order to commit him to a hospital, since it sounds as if he is potentially dangerous to himself and others. Consult your family doctor or lawyer, your brother's pastor or present counselor (assuming he has one), or the local mental health organization to learn how this can be done. Usually, the parties concerned must contact a judge to secure a court directive that requests the mentally disturbed person to a private or state hospital. This secures reliable treatment for a period of thirty to ninety days, time enough to reinstate proper medication for your brother.

Most people with schizophrenia are reluctant to take their medicine. Some refuse it outright because they don't want to admit their need for assistance (a paranoid trait). If this becomes habitual, there is usually very little family members can do about it—which is all the more reason why a schizophrenic who is out of control should not be living at home. Your brother, specifically, needs professional treatment and constant supervision until he is stabilized. This can best be handled if he is hospitalized, at least temporarily.

Can schizophrenia be treated without medication? If so, how is this done?

As was mentioned above, schizophrenia is the result of a physiological malfunction—a chemical imbalance of a neurotransmitter in the brain called *dopamine.* This substance floats between the brain cells and transmits information from one brain cell to the next. In the limbic system of the brain, it controls logical thinking and regular thought patterns. Since an imbalance of dopamine leads to disorientation and disjointed thinking, schizophrenics may hear voices, experience visual illusions, or imagine other things that are untrue.

Any chemical imbalance is virtually impossible to treat without medicine. It would be like saying to someone with hypothyroidism, "Come on, snap out of your fatigue and negative thinking." Schizophrenics require a combination of medical treatment and loving, supportive care through counseling. They should especially be protected from stressful situations and nontranquil environments, which tend to worsen their symptoms.

Before the discovery of certain medications, people who developed schizophrenia suffered with its symptoms for life. Very rarely did anyone recover from the illness spontaneously. Now, with the use of medications that correct the dopamine imbalance (e.g., Thorazine, Mellaril, Stelazine, Navane), partial and sometimes complete recovery is possible for many people who would otherwise spend the rest of their lives in mental hospitals. If treatment for schizophrenia is started within three to six months of the first outbreak of symptoms, some patients are able to do well without medication later on. But most will need to see a psychiatrist monthly or quarterly for the rest of their lives. (For a detailed explanation of schizophrenia, consult our textbook, *Introduction to Psychology and Counseling*, [Baker 1982, 1991]).

How is the "histrionic personality" developed, and what are some signs that these traits are getting out of hand?

1. Like all personality types, histrionic personality traits are partially inherited, but largely the result of environmental factors during early years. Personal choices are also a factor. Many, but not all, histrionics were sexually abused or had poor relationships with the parent of the opposite sex. Two-thirds of histrionic personalities were *ignored* by the parent of the opposite sex so the child developed a more than normal craving for the attention of the opposite sex. The child discovered which behaviors attracted the attention of the opposite sex and worked hard to develop these traits. Many histrionics become singers, musicians, cheerleaders, actors, evangelists, and salespersons. They tend to become performers.

2. Girls who were ignored often grow up feeling inferior, and become seductive to get the attention of a male (toward whom they usually have a deep root of bitterness). They frequently hold grudges toward men for being inattentive—because they were deprived of a normal relationship with their father. As adults they still crave the attention of the opposite sex, but unconsciously want to prove that men are untrustworthy, just like their fathers were. Proverbs 5 describes the histrionic female.

3. The male histrionic has generally the same behavior

pattern. Deep down he craves his mother's absent affections and resents her, so he has an affair with a female to get even with his mother, while getting attention at the same time to fill his mother-vacuum.

4. About one-third of histrionics come from homes where they grew up as the favorite child. One child may be treated as "special," and is allowed to get away with "everything." This same child later feels like he or she is "entitled" and deserves everything, because of a resulting combination of sociopathic and histrionic traits.

Histrionics have to be on guard that they don't tempt others to fall into sexual sin. Satan knows our personality types, and he'll tempt us when we are weak. The obsessive will be tempted to be overly concerned about control and financial issues. The histrionic will be tempted with sexual desires or other lusts of the flesh (food, alcohol, and drug addictions).

Histrionics must realize that they use their surface emotions as a defense against deeper emotions. Having an emotional surface structure can be both positive and negative. The negative aspects are obvious: being overly sensitive and particularly subjective. But when histrionics come to terms with bitterness that has resulted perhaps from an unsatisfied craving for parental attention, such surface emotions will be much less likely to trip them up. On the positive side, histrionics have charisma and are talented at influencing other people. The apostle Peter was a histrionic personality.

Histrionic personality types must be led to deal with their bitterness and to learn forgiveness. When this is accomplished, the tendency toward sexual sin diminishes significantly. Instead, they develop respect for themselves and others in the eyes of God as cherished persons who must be free from the bondage of improper relationships.

Another aspect of the histrionic personality type is hypochondria—headaches, backaches, and other aches and pains. Research reveals that many humans somaticize (subconsciously make themselves sick), but histrionic personalities have especially strong tendencies toward this. They typically base their outlook on how they feel.

Histrionic personalities also tend toward religious systems that overemphasize healing physical symptoms, and having emotional experiences—how one feels—more than on basing worship on a clear understanding of God's Word. For example, if you ask them if they are saved, histrionics first decide if they feel saved. If they don't feel saved, they may think they're not. After another emotional worship experience they may "feel" saved again, instead of trusting God's Word, which teaches everlasting salvation, sealed until the day of redemption (Eph. 1).

Histrionic traits are common; overcoming them is not. This is not to say that histrionic traits are impossible to correct, but to state the fact that this performance-oriented personality type is highly rewarded in society and many are reluctant to mature out of the unhealthy aspects of it. The apostle Peter (a histrionic) did choose to mature in Christ and even died a martyr's death eventually. Many believers gain insights into their dysfunctional family backgrounds, attention-seeking motives, impulsiveness and pride, and—like Peter—decide to grow in Christ. A mature Peter was probably still histrionic in a healthy sense: fun to be with, maturely emotional, with godly charisma and charm. We look forward to meeting him in heaven. But this kind of growth requires a humble willingness to look at one's own deceitful heart and human depravity, step by step as the Holy Spirit reveals the truth about love hunger and sinful ways used to fill it in the past. God wants to fill such hunger with himself, through intimate bonding and fellowship with him and fellow believers—especially mature believers who are willing to confront them lovingly when unhealthy histrionic traits are exhibited.

Other common personality types are the sociopathic, paranoid, and passive-aggressive personalities. Sociopaths (antisocial personalities) are usually adults who were "spoiled" as children. Their parents did not adequately discipline them or teach them to get along with others. All humans are born with primarily sociopathic, self-centered tendencies. Love and discipline help us mute our naturally selfish inclinations to use and manipulate others. Children left to their own pleasures will eventually shame their parents. Solomon was aware of this a few thousand years ago.

Severely abused children may also become more sociopathic (antisocial) as adults because of rage toward authority figures in general. However, many verbally and physically abused children develop paranoid personalities with lack of trust, a need to be in control, repressed hostility, prejudices, and rigid thinking. Because they often choose to run their own businesses, they often become very successful financially.

Passive-aggressive personalities are overly dependent people whose parents made too many decisions for them while they were growing up. These people stuff their anger toward the dominant parent and spend the rest of their lives subconsciously getting even with that parent by being late, pouting, procrastinating, stubbornness, inefficiency, setting themselves up for failure, and dependence on drugs, alcohol, or food. Passive-aggressives expect others to bail them out. With God's help and with long-term Christian counseling, all of the personality types can mature toward Christ-likeness.

All of the personality types are discussed in more detail in our book, *An Introduction to Christian Psychology*, (Baker, 1982, 1991).

7

Practical Handling of Some Complicated Problems

Professionals in the field of psychology are not limited to compiling dry facts and scientific theories about mental and emotional processes. Their underlying concern is with human *behavior*, which is often linked to "inner motivation"—the sum total of one's genetic makeup and life experiences (including personal choices), especially those of early childhood. Psychological counseling is based not on "mysterious" guesswork but on verifiable studies of observable behavior and emotional response. This book presents a cross section of the types of questions most frequently asked of professionals in the mental-health field. The situations and characters may differ, but the basic focus of each question is the same: how to achieve personal contentment and fulfilling relationships.

In this section the emphasis will be on suggesting prac-

127

tical ways to approach some not uncommon behavior maladjustments or emotional overreactions. You will notice that some of these topics have been mentioned previously. For these repetitions, our aim is to present still another angle or viewpoint. While questions about mental health keep coming to us in a steady stream, many are interrelated. As previously mentioned, we believe that God is at the center of every solution. Psychological theory and medical know-how are important in treating people's emotional ills, but only inasmuch as they dovetail with the purpose and mind of God. And, as is usually the case with human behavior, God's plan leads us to practical answers.

My mother-in-law has an "anxiety disease" known as "agoraphobia"—that is, she fears leaving her home. Even though she is a Christian, she avoids church attendance. She is also very domineering and manipulative. Through the years we have given in to her ways, but this is having negative effects on our children. Our whole family is building hostility toward her. How should we react to her in a healthy way, for her sake and our own?

"Disease" is not the most accurate description for your mother-in-law's agoraphobia, because it is quite likely a problem with no organic basis. It is better called a psychological disorder. Being "domineering" is one of the key elements of this maladjustment because it is a way to compensate for underlying feelings of inferiority (insecurity) and the anxiety they evoke.

Some people compensate for their low self-esteem by feeding what Scripture calls "the lust of the flesh" (1 John 2:16), which may include something as subtle as overeating, or as excessive as acting out sexual fantasies. Others give in to "the lust of the eyes" (materialism) and try to buy happiness. Still others are caught up in "the boastful pride of life" (NASB). This includes continual struggles for power, prestige, and control. In your mother-in-law's case, her basic insecurity has made her avoid leaving the safe and protective familiarity of her home. Her attempt to dominate family members is her way of proving that, at least at home, she has a certain amount of "status." Your mother-in-law might have an obsessive-compulsive personality. Many of the people treated for agoraphobia and other severe anxiety disorders are the oldest child of their sex in their families and have a propensity toward certain obsessive-compulsive behavior, better known as perfectionism. She was probably the victim of verbal abuse and conditional acceptance as a child. She must have suffered some severe emotional pains in her life because she is so afraid to lose control or to socialize. Pray that God will give her the courage to get professional help for this serious problem. She may require four to six weeks of intensive hospital therapy. Show her compassion and focus on her good traits. Clearly, perfectionists have some positive traits, such as being hard-working, conscientious, and dedicated. But counterbalancing these pluses are some hard-to-tolerate minuses, not the least of which is a need to manipulate people and circumstances.

If your mother-in-law *is* a perfectionist, her problems probably date back to her upbringing. This is not said to lay blame on her parents. Incidentally, too much time is wasted on fruitless efforts to "find fault." The *final* goal of constructive therapy is to fix what is broken, not figure out how it was broken in the first place. Nonetheless, weeds must be dealt with at the roots, and emotional disorders frequently stem from childhood experiences.

During and after hospital therapy, a Christian psychologist or psychiatrist can help your mother-in-law uncover her hidden problems and conflicts. As she learns why she feels insecure, she will recognize her unconscious urge to control. Through emotional and spiritual growth, she can find peace and will eventually be able to back off and have more fun without being so controlling.

How your mother-in-law behaves is *her* assignment, but how you react to her is yours. You must decide that the most important thing for you is knowing and loving God, loving your husband and children, and enjoying the abundant life that Jesus has given you (John 10). From that perspective, it is a sin for you to allow your mother-in-law to create tension, anxiety, sadness, and hard feelings in your family life.

You may be thinking, "But the Bible says to honor your mother and father." Yes, you must remain polite and considerate, keeping her at a distance if necessary. Avoid arguments, but be assertive with her—that is, don't let her step beyond certain bounds. Speak plainly to her, but always in respectful tones. Make it clear that your family is under God's control. Although you are to act in love and kindness, do not allow your mother-in-law to jeopardize your immediate family's unity and peace. If she becomes angry over your new resistance to her manipulation, this is *her* problem.

Hospitalization for an agoraphobic may be as frightening as jumping out of a plane with a parachute. She will fear trusting a hospital staff to "control" her. Encourage her, remind her that agoraphobia is a curable disorder, and pray that God will give her the courage to get the treatment she must painfully work through to get well.

You cannot allow your mother-in-law's behavior to affect your decision to let God lead you. Just forgive her, and help lower your children's expectations of their grandmother without demeaning her in any way. Tell them, "Grandma has her good traits and bad traits, as we all do. Here's what you can expect and not expect. But always remember that she loves us." This helps minimize their disappointment or personal hurts. Your children can learn honor, respect, and love by watching examples of how you apply biblical principles to your relationship with your husband's mother and your own parents.

Is there such a thing as a "shopaholic"? I can't seem to stop spending money, and I have several large credit-card debts. Why does this happen to me? How can I control it?

A "shopaholic," or spending addict, has succumbed to "lust of the eyes"—one of the three main areas in which people are tempted by Satan. When juxtaposed with the teaching of Scripture to love not "the world or anything in the world?" (1 John 2:15), the vice of overspending appears to be more a spiritual failing than a mental or emotional disorder.

Psychiatric research shows that all human beings experience feelings of inferiority and self-doubt to some degree. This is especially true of people who are apart from Christ. As previously mentioned, some people go through life trying to overcome their low self-worth through "the lust of the flesh" (sexual fantasies or behavior or indulgence of other physical appetites), "lust of the eyes" (materialism), and the "boastful pride of life" (power struggles and status seeking). (See 1 John 2:16 NASB).

Unwise spending is one way people try to compensate for their feelings of inferiority. The ability to spend money and have possessions is personally gratifying, but careless spending is not only wasteful—it's sinful. If the insecurity that fuels the urge to spend is unresolved, shopping can become addictive. The end result may be financial ruin or clinical depression—or both. Resolving your root insecurities is the most important action you can take to overcome "shopaholism." You may require insight-oriented outpatient counseling for several months.

A balanced, common-sense view of personal finance is also what you need, especially in your use of credit. It is easy to think of buying on credit as receiving something for free, since no cash changes hands at the time. But payoff day always comes around eventually. Because credit cards give a feeling of power and a false sense of security, they can create problems for many people. If you hope to control your credit-card buying rather than have *it* control you, pay bills off in full each month. Using credit cards *only* for the sake of convenience reflects a much more balanced view and wiser use of credit. Better yet, don't use them at all—pay immediately by cash or check.

Overcoming your shopaholism begins with preparing a personal budget and doing your best to stay within it. First, determine to live on 80 percent of your take-home pay, and no more. Then allot 10 percent of your after-tax earnings to the church. If you want to give more than that, give from the 80 percent. Scripture does not *command* that you tithe, but there is plenty of scriptural support for giving your "firstfruits" to your local church. Place the remaining 10 percent of your take-home pay in a savings account, bank CD, or another safe form of investment that provides a fair return on your money. Keep some of your savings in a form you can easily access for emergencies, to avoid penalties for early withdrawal. (There are some very basic concepts about personal finances in our book, *The Money Diet*, [Baker, 1985]).

Your main goal in life should be to serve Jesus Christ. If you are constantly worried about finances, Satan is using this to weaken your faith and debilitate your spirits. It is a sin to be in bondage to money! If you find that living on 80 percent of your income is not possible, change your lifestyle. This may mean you'll have to make some "sacrifices." Recognize that many items you may think of as *necessary* for your happiness are really just frivolous luxuries.

Impulsive spenders need practice at rationally thinking through their buying habits. They need to protect themselves by planning their spending ahead of time. And they especially need to consider what specifically motivates them to spend to excess. Insight-oriented Christian therapy will enable you to discover what root problems "drive" your spending addiction.

Some people spend for revenge or rebellion. If, for example, they grew up in a home where their parents "counted sheets of toilet tissue and spanked us for not turning out all the lights," as one shopaholic commented, they might have an unconscious urge to spend lavishly in defiance of childhood rules. Others spend to rebel against their autocratic mates, or to get even with them for being irresponsible in some other way. (Of course, this violates Romans 12:17–21, which says that revenge belongs to God alone.)

Other overspenders grew up in poverty, deprived of the basic necessities. As adults they can go in either of two directions. They may become miserly and stingy, in the hope that frugality alone will protect them from ever being in want again. On the other hand, they may go to the opposite extreme and buy-buy-buy everything they never had as a child. Running through this philosophy is often the idea that material possessions define one's self-worth.

Sociopaths who have shopaholic tendencies are in another category altogether. They simply spend—as they do everything—without a conscience. Spending/buying feels good to them. These types can be especially clever about borrowing other people's money to fulfill their feel-good habit. They feel entitled to use others, so they continually rip people off. The cyclothymic personality—the person who quite often feels on a high—usually has impaired judgment and can go through a long binge of spending before "awakening" to reality, which often precipitates a down period.

In all cases of shopaholism, however, the application of biblical principles and dedication to personal discipline is a major key to successfully overcoming the problem. You may need to face up to leftover feelings from childhood and verbalize them, especially when you feel the urge to spend. Share these feelings with your husband and with the Lord in prayer. Ask God to help you see what is triggering your desire to spend and to help you control these urges.

Disciplining yourself to *never* buy impulsively requires that you budget only a small allowance for personal shopping and always use a shopping list. When you want to make an expensive purchase, pray about it while waiting at least twenty-four hours before buying. Ask yourself if the primary motivation for buying is immediate gratification rather than long-term utility. Ask God if the purchase pleases him. Is it what he wants for you? Once you have determined that it fits your budget and you feel comfortable about making the purchase, go ahead and enjoy it.

Interestingly enough, spending is often the emotional crutch that Christians lean on to feel better about themselves, because it is one area they consider to be outside the spiritual realm. A lack of self-control in one area, however, usually leads to temptation and excess in others, such as power struggles, sexual sins, or overeating. The root of insecurity that feeds these problems must be removed before any real, lasting peace can be achieved.

Helpful books on the subject of overcoming insecurity include *The Sensation of Being Somebody* by Maurice Wagner (Zondervan, 1985) and *His Image, My Image* by Josh McDowell (Here's Life, 1985). Overcoming shopaholism requires balance in attitude and motivation, both of which necessitate deepening your personal relationship with the Lord.

I have battled many fears and worries since my parents were divorced when I was seven years old. Since losing my job four months ago and moving away from my family, my fear of being alone has worsened. (I am a single adult.) How can I overcome my anxieties?

There are several common-sense solutions that are helpful for overcoming fear of specific situations and reducing one's general level of anxiety.

You quite likely have unresolved conflicts from the past. During your parents' divorce you probably had fears about the future and conflicts about the family situation that have carried over into adulthood. Young children typically feel a heavy burden of insecurity when their parents are fighting, and that weight is intensified by divorce. No doubt this explains some of the residual fear you are experiencing now. It is unusual, however, for adults to feel such extreme tension about being physically separated from family members. This may eventually require counseling, especially since you must first understand why you have developed such a collection of fears.

Next you need to build a support system in your new environment. Everyone needs the encouragement found in the company of friends. In a new city the surroundings and people are unfamiliar and you are probably lonely. Develop friendships with people your age who can share your joys and ease your disappointments—people you can identify with. If you have already joined a church, and it offers little in the way of fellowship, consider finding another that does. Christian friends are an invaluable source of strength.

You also need to take action to find a job, since financial concerns are probably part of your worries. Look for a roommate to share expenses, making sure, of course, that she is trustworthy and reliable. If you are not already busy trying to find work, begin immediately. Even if you don't need the income, work is a healthy way to fill your days, and it will take you away from the routine of being locked up with your negative emotions.

Unless you can learn to handle your fears, you could be headed for clinical depression. This may mean you would need to enter therapy, in which case a psychiatrist would probably prescribe a nonaddicting antidepressant medication (if there is a physiological component to your depression). However, except for manic-depressive illness, medication is generally used as a short-term measure. Anxiety and depression grow from deep inner feelings that must be squarely faced. Ventilating and talking about your fears in counseling is an important step toward personal peace.

Behavioral techniques might also help. Fear breeds worry, and worry breeds more fear. This cycle must be broken if you are to get better. Learn to see anxiety as a signal meant to help you calm down and face what is worrying you. When fear rises up against you, take action. Identify the specific source of your fear and then decide what you can do to correct the situation. For example, if

you are worried about your physical health, consult a doctor to assure yourself that nothing is wrong—or to be
treated, if that is necessary. If finances are your concern
at the moment, consider whether you have done all you
can to relieve that pressure, as suggested above. Carry a
Bible with you, and read it to encourage you through the
struggle. Keep it at your bedside to help you through
lonely nights. Philippians 4:6 says, "Be anxious for nothing . . ." (NASB). Scripture memorization and meditation
can make a great difference, when combined with self-
help measures to correct whatever fear-producing factors
are causing you emotional pain.

It is possible to become totally overcome by anxiety.
This is known as an *anxiety* (or panic) *attack*, which is
usually manifest by disturbing physiological symptoms,
including rapid heartbeat, shortness of breath, and sweat-
ing. If you ever experience such symptoms, contact your
physician or psychiatrist immediately. You may need hospitalization to recover properly, and there may be factors
other than anxiety that are causing the reactions.

Anxiety is like the tide; it comes and goes because of
unseen pressure. When the tide is high, your inner pressures have increased through neglect. However, do not be
fooled by a falling tide. Unless you confront the cause of
your anxiety, the high water of fear will be back.

***Two years ago, my wife and I began having marital
problems. One morning I woke up feeling like my mind
was outside of my body. I'm seeing a psychiatrist now,
but I still feel strangely "disconnected" quite often.
What is happening to me? Is it likely to be permanent?***

You are experiencing *depersonalization*. This mental
phenomenon is fairly common in the teenage years, but
more rare in adults, and often results from feelings of inferiority and stress. One of the sensations that commonly
accompanies this condition is feeling detached from one's
body. Since teenagers often deal with self-doubt and inse-

curity, they may encounter some depersonalization during times of pressure. Should this condition be debilitating or recurring, however, counseling is necessary to rebuild one's confidence.

Part of the solution in your case is to learn how to be your own best friend. Begin to look at yourself the way God looks at you—as a worthwhile human being. When you really begin to like yourself and recognize your good qualities and your position in Christ, the feelings of insecurity and depersonalization will fade. Most importantly, be assured that these sensations can be overcome.

Frequently there are underlying issues that spawn this condition. Perhaps something specific has caused the marital problems you mention. Can you recall a recent event at home or at work that shattered your self-respect? God wants us to have a healthy kind of pride in ourselves (see Gal. 6:4)—self-esteem that is based on our position as his child, and the fact that we are becoming more like Christ every day. (This is not to be a *false* pride, however, which tempts us to believe we are better than others.) If you can identify what injured your "healthy pride," you can begin to confront your insecurity with the reinforcement of God's loving perspective of you. You can probably improve your marital relationship in the process.

Studying has always been a problem for me, whether it pertains to Scripture, prayer, or academics. I can easily spend 50–70 percent of my time daydreaming instead of studying. Is this problem physical or psychological—and how can I deal with it?

At least five possibilities should be considered in reference to your inability to concentrate:

1. You may have an *attention-deficit disorder.* While this generally affects children (see chapter 5), some adults do not completely grow out of it and may continue to have occasional residual hyperactivity and diminished attention span.

2. Hidden *anxiety* may be present. Evaluate your current pressures. Since your problem has persisted for a long time, you might consider a past fear or stress that has gone unresolved.

3. *Depression* is a possible explanation. One of the main symptoms we look for when we suspect clinical depression is poor concentration. Other symptoms that can accompany depression include feelings of deep sadness, trouble sleeping, and appetite changes.

4. A *schizophrenic process* could be developing. Preferring to daydream rather than live in the real world is an early warning sign of mental illness.

5. You may have a *physical problem.* Your first step is to get a complete medical examination to rule out any organic causes for your lack of concentration. Then see a psychiatrist for a mental evaluation. Problems with the brain or nervous system can frequently show up in the form of memory lapses or inattentiveness. The psychiatrist may want to refer you to a neurologist if it appears that you need a more complete neurological check-up.

If no physiological or mental disorders are found, seek Christian counseling either as an inpatient or outpatient. The aim is for you to confront any hurtful memories you may have been carrying since childhood. Your local mental health organization or pastor may know of some competent Christian counselors in your area or call 1-800-545-1819 for the location of the nearest Minirth-Meier Clinic.

I have been married to a considerate and loving man for six years. Recently I've been troubled with recurring sexual fantasies that are anything but gentle and tender. These thoughts involve my husband, but tend to come up during our intimate moments. Sometimes they occur when I am alone. This troubles me. I don't know what effect these fantasies may have on our healthy marriage, my personal psyche, or my Christian walk. How can I deal with this problem? Would it be advisable to tell my husband what's going on?

You have some very realistic and practical concerns here. There are several things that you might consider.

First of all, sexual fantasizing is "normal" to a certain degree. This doesn't make it right, even if the daydreams involve one's spouse. Since sinful thoughts do enter our minds, the key issue is how we deal with them. Once we have an ungodly thought, we are responsible for handling it. Scripture promises that Christ can help us overcome any temptation (1 Cor. 10:13). This is the proper attitude to have when facing sexual temptations and any unwelcome thoughts.

You can find immediate relief by replacing those thoughts with memorized Scripture. Meditating on passages in the Song of Solomon can help you focus on healthy sexual expression. Quote these verses when your fantasies appear. There is most likely nothing "perverted" about your sexual daydreams. God intended marital intimacy to be a source of joy and pleasure for both partners. If sexual love between you and your husband is not fulfilling for you, it may be beneficial to communicate this to him.

The fantasies may indicate an unresolved problem between you and your husband. The underlying conflict might not be sexual in nature, even though it is manifesting itself in the sexual area. These thoughts could be a passive way for you to express some ambivalence and confusion over a completely different issue. The issue may even be a control issue or some unresolved anger toward someone.

Whether or not you should tell your husband depends on several factors. You should share feelings that may strain your relationship *only* if doing so will be helpful to both of you and will resolve a problem. Timing and the way you bring up the matter are important considerations. Your husband may not be able to handle hearing this if it implies a criticism of his lovemaking. You know your mate better than anyone, and you alone are in the best position to make the decision about telling him— and, more importantly, *how* to tell him in a loving way.

A friend of mine recently committed suicide. I was shocked, taken completely by surprise. What signs can I look for that indicate a person is likely to commit suicide? How could I help such a person?

There are several warning signs of suicide:

1. *Severe depression.* A risk of suicide is present if a person feels blue, sad, hopeless, or cries a lot; is tired or sleepless; has noticeable weight changes. Be aware that 15 percent of people who suffer from clinical depression commit suicide.
2. *Talking about suicide.* These "threats" should be taken very seriously and are often cries for help.
3. *Chronic illness.* Even when an illness is not considered terminal, people who have endured long-term pain and/or are incapacitated often want an end to their suffering, even if it means death.
4. *Isolation and loneliness.* Elderly people, singles, and alienated adolescents may have suicidal tendencies if they are isolated from the companionship of others.
5. Signs of *painful thinking* or *severe emotional pain.* An example would be the intense hopelessness that is often seen after a significant loss, such as the death of a spouse or loss of a job.
6. *Severe stress.* An excess of disturbing life events within a short period of time can precipitate a suicide attempt.
7. *Intense need to achieve.* Ironically, this may be exhibited in chronic self-destructive behavior (e.g., alcoholism).
8. *Prior history of suicide attempts (or threats).*

Suicidal individuals often follow a pattern, beginning with fleeting thoughts of suicide that are awarded increasing consideration until an actual suicide attempt is made.

Depression is the leading cause of suicide—which is the tenth leading cause of death in the United States.

Since over 10 percent of the persons who make a suicide gesture eventually follow through, anyone who threatens to take his or her own life should be taken seriously, even though many such threats are basically manipulative in nature. About 8 percent of those who do commit suicide had warned someone of their intentions.

The suicide rate is higher among the divorced or widowed and in the upper socioeconomic groups; it is most common among single, white adult males over forty-five years of age. Although women *attempt* suicide five times more frequently than men, twice as many men actually succeed. The probable reason is that men tend to use a more violent means of suicide, such as a firearm or car crash, while women defer to a more moderate and less foolproof method, such as drug overdose. (Women may also be more apt to use suicide as a manipulative gesture because of cultural influences.)

Individuals who exhibit suicidal tendencies usually need professional counseling to change their self-destructive thoughts and behavior.Of the seven suicides recorded in Scripture, none of the perpetrators was in the will of God at the time of his death. The biblical examples of suicide are:

Abimelech (Judg. 9:54)   Samson (Judg. 16:30)
Saul (1 Sam. 31:4)   Saul's armor-bearer
Ahithophel (2 Sam. 17:23)   (1 Sam. 31:5)
Judas (Matt. 27:3–5)   Zimri (1 Kings 16:18)

In situations where someone is seriously considering suicide, prompt intervention is vital. Encourage anyone in this condition to check into the behavioral-medicine unit of a Christian psychiatric facility. If this is not an option, try to get the person to any hospital emergency room. If he or she will not cooperate, you may need to alert the police or other authorities. Although this may prompt a negative reaction on the part of the very one you are trying to help, you can be encouraged by the fact that many suicidal individuals are inwardly crying out for love and want to be stopped.

We would encourage you to not feel guilty for your friend's suicide. No one but God can read minds, and false guilt is common after the kind of loss you recently experienced.

People are supposed to be happy around the holidays, especially at Christmas. Why do I feel so sad when everything should be going well during these special times?

Actually, it is quite common for people to become somewhat depressed during the holidays. Television makes everyone look extremely happy on Thanksgiving and Christmas specials and people naturally wonder why they aren't feeling that way. As we remember the traditions and joy of past celebrations and grieve again for missing loved ones, present circumstances suffer by comparison. The expected letdown after celebrating any long-awaited event contributes to depression as well.

Holidays bring related pressures, such as getting stuck in traffic for hours during the shopping rush, and having less money to spend on presents than we hoped. Loneliness pinches harder when great emphasis is placed on celebrating with family and loved ones, since that is not always possible in our mobile society.

Here are some specific suggestions for reducing holiday depression:

Try to look accurately at past holidays. Ecclesiastes 7:10 says, "Do not say, 'Why were the old days better than these?' For it is not wise to ask such questions." All of us tend to look at the past as the "good old days." Some may easily forget and minimize the problems and hurts of the past, assuming that present difficulties are the worst and the only ones that matter.

Give all your holiday expectations to God. Realize that life itself, especially at Christmas, is not to be centered on people and circumstances, but on the Lord. If we will realize that God's perspective is eternal, the little things that go wrong in the few years we have on earth pale in significance. Then they can be dealt with more easily.

Be aware of the false images that come from the media. We all have inferiority feelings, and Satan appeals to them through material enticements, sensuality, and commercialism. These are all part of the world's system, and we must not buy into it. Christmas has meaning only when we worship Christ and strengthen our love relationship with him.

Remember your priorities in the holiday schedule. Don't be afraid to turn down invitations. Staying disciplined in your eating and sleeping habits will protect your spiritual attitude. Many people wear themselves out during the Christmas season. Make a list of the specific plans you definitely want to keep over the holidays—and cut out the others.

Face holiday-related emotional issues. Perhaps you suffered the loss of a loved one during a previous Christmas season. Then, each time Christmas comes around again, you are reminded of the grief and loss of that tragic event. You may need to spend time alone and have a good cry. On the other hand, you might want to share your burden with a friend. A burden shared becomes only half a burden. Don't be afraid to open up to a few people whom you know you can trust.

Keep the celebration within sensible financial limits. You don't need to spend a small fortune on Christmas gifts. The Bible tells us to "Set your minds on things above, not on earthly things" (Col. 3:2).

Deal with loneliness directly. If you are lonely, develop a specific plan to deal with it. Consider people who need you during the holidays. Visit a shut-in, offer to babysit so a harried young mother can do some shopping, volunteer at a soup kitchen—and so on.

Make the holiday a time to start memorizing Scripture. It may be especially helpful to memorize specific verses concerning Christmas, but any passage that encourages and strengthens you will do.

I am approaching retirement and seem to have many more worries and concerns than in earlier years. Life seems to be so complicated now, and I don't have the energy of my younger days. What are some problems I should anticipate as part of the aging process?

The retirement years present a unique set of problems that must be recognized by those approaching the later years of life:

Loneliness. Spouses die, and adult children may live afar. (Since women generally live longer than men, there are more widows than widowers.)

Marital problems. Traditionally it has been believed that elderly couples cannot enjoy sex. But God has blessed sex in marriage, and it should be enjoyed throughout the years. This is only one potential problem in marriages of longevity. There are others. For example, the burden of caring for an ailing spouse may tax the strength and patience of even the most loving partner. In other cases, a decades-long marriage may be threatened by one partner's concern that life is fast-fleeting and not much has been accomplished as planned. It may seem that there is so little to look forward to that "one last fling" may be the unfortunate solution.

Economic problems. The average financial status of individuals over the age of sixty-five has improved in recent times, but many are still forced to live on a reduced, fixed income. Some of our country's elderly are forced to enter nursing homes, a financial drain on private savings that may leave a spouse impoverished. Retirement for some can mean a loss of status in society.

Psychological problems. Aging can bring the loss of self-esteem, impairment of memory, and a narrowing of interest. Dependency on others is difficult to accept, especially when brought on by fading abilities and physical weakness. Some cope with this by becoming hyper-independent and cantankerous as families wrestle with the problem of where an elderly loved one should live (home nursing facility, etc.). Unhealthy coping defenses, such as regression, giving up, withdrawal, and projection (accusing others of having their faults) may show up.

Physical problems. Life expectancies have increased because of medical progress, but physical problems still await the elderly. Old age can bring diminished sharpness of the senses, decreased muscle mass and motor strength, arthritis, and a general decline in the function of internal organs. The risk of such organic illnesses as diabetes, heart disease, hypertension, glaucoma, and cancer is greater in the elderly, despite advances in prevention and treatment.

Mental problems. Depression is the most common psychological disorder in older people. This may be a straightforward type of depression—sad facial expression and hopeless thinking. More often it is masked, yet revealed by such symptoms as repeated health worries, sleep disturbances, appetite loss, energy depletion, back pain, and extreme concern over bodily functions (e.g., bowel movements). Unfortunately, depression frequently leads to suicide in people over sixty-five.

"Senility" affects many elderly people. A decrease in brain function can cause loss of recent memory, emotions that are easily triggered, and impaired mental ability. Judgment and reasoning capacities may deteriorate.These symptoms can be caused by a hardening of the arteries leading to the brain (cerebral arteriosclerosis), but most so-called senility is due to Alzheimer's disease. The exact cause of Alzheimer's is not known, but some believe it involves a neurotransmitter known as acetylcholine. Alzheimer's usually sets in after age 70 but may begin much earlier. While its onset is gradual, the disease becomes steadily progressive and usually results in death within ten years.

Drug dependency is another problem of old age. To cope with stress and depression, many of our country's aging are turning to alcohol, sleeping pills, and tranquilizers.

For more complete examination of the problems of the elderly and a study of the aging process, see *Beating the Clock* (Baker, 1985).

My health is worsening as I advance in age, and I often feel lonely and purposeless. What can I do to take care of myself and make sure my days can be lived to their fullest?

While advancing age presents many problems (as discussed above), there are also many helps available, particularly for the Christian.

General physical and medical care can make life more enjoyable. Annual physical examinations are especially important for senior citizens—to monitor the health of physiological functions, uncover hidden signs of disease processes, and review the effectiveness of medications already prescribed. For women, regular mammograms will increase the chances of discovering malignancies of the breast early enough for successful treatment. Appropriate exercise, as outlined by your personal physician, can improve energy level. A healthy diet—especially one that is high in fiber and bulk—can keep blood sugar in better balance and reduce constipation. Habitual use of laxatives should be avoided, but stool softeners such as natural vegetable fiber can be helpful. Reducing fat intake, quitting smoking, and eliminating alcohol are, of course, easy ways to avoid two of life's major killers at any age.

Seek the advice of competent medical professionals and follow their directions. If a doctor says that some popularized, unproven "cure" is suspect, believe the warning and avoid the potential danger. Always seek a second opinion before undergoing a major treatment or surgical procedure of any kind.

We all need love, acceptance, and the moral support of

others. As individuals age they gain valuable experience and therefore have much to offer young people. Grandparenting is one of the greatest joys of life creating a profound cross-generational bond that enlightens a child's understanding of life in the context of time and enriches an older person's days in the process. If your grandchildren live far away, maintaining contact with phone calls, cards, letters, and photo sharing will help you renew that bond when you do exchange visits. Even if you have no grandchildren, there is an opportunity for this type of sharing in the "surrogate grandparenting" programs sponsored by many local organizations. Or there may be a friendly family right in your neighborhood who would be very happy to welcome you into their home.

Older couples who are having marital difficulties should seek help through their pastors and other counselors. Most problems can be resolved if both partners are willing to accept realistic solutions. How wonderful it is when a couple demonstrates love through the late years of life! Of course, if your beloved partner is no longer with you, you will cherish the precious memories of your years together. But don't dwell in the past. He or she would have wanted you to find happiness on your own, with new friendships and interests.

Retirement often enables parents to have increased contact with their adult children, which is usually welcomed if it is not overdone. On the other hand, some aging parents express strong preferences for remaining completely independent of their children. To enjoy a rich family life in one's older years, a proper balance must be found when it comes to time spent together. In particular, too much "advice giving" by either generation can undermine the relationship.

Enjoying the support of friends and neighbors is a plus of the retirement years, when there is more time for community activities. Regular attendance at church increases the opportunity for fellowship with others, as does participating in the programs of senior-citizen groups found in most communities.

Membership in the American Association of Retired Persons provides access to extensive resources, discounts, and services. This can begin as early as age fifty, and it will help you prepare for advancing age and retirement. For more information, write to AARP, Membership Processing Center, 215 Long Beach Blvd., Long Beach, CA 90801.

Church membership presents a terrific opportunity for mutual service and encouragement. Senior adults have much to offer the church. Even if weaker physically, they are often strong in wisdom. This makes them a critical part of the body of Christ. Perhaps your church has a special program for the elderly (if not, ask your pastor about getting one started). You and others your age must participate if it is to be successful. But remember that you are welcome in so many other church activities, regardless of how old you are!

A burden shared is only half a burden. You will no doubt benefit from sharing your personal disappointments with an empathetic friend. If you become generally depressed, professional psychotherapy is needed to orient you to the problems of your present environment. Deep insight-oriented therapy would probably be unnecessary unless you have long-standing emotional problems not yet resolved.

Benefits for the elderly—Social Security, Medicare, Medicaid, among others—must be considered as part of your resource package. Government at national, state, and local levels, as well as churches and other organizations, provide a variety of services for older persons. Many communities have a Meals-on-Wheels program, which brings hot meals to the residence of those who are housebound. Many communities publish a directory of such services. If the time comes when you can no longer live alone, a wide variety of housing alternatives is available for the elderly, ranging from government-subsidized apartments to life-care facilities.

Purpose and activity are vital to happy, healthy living—at any age. Staying active mentally and physically was the "fountain of youth" for such productive seniors as Rubinstein, Schweitzer, Michelangelo, Churchill, and a host of others. Consider the special skills, knowledge, or talents you might share with others, since many organizations, churches, and colleges make extensive use of elderly volunteer staff members.

Finally, seek help in Scripture meditation and prayer. A person's mature years provide a splendid time for the deepening of a satisfying walk with God.

Addictive Behavior

Substance abuse and eating disorders are growing menaces in society today. Depending on mood-changing drugs or food to provide security or relieve anxiety is addictive, unhealthy, and self-defeating. Scripture teaches us to rely on Christ to satisfy all our longings and meet our every need.

Once an eating disorder or a chemical addiction begins, the physiological and/or psychological dependency that follows can be difficult to overcome—especially alone. Anyone experiencing problems with drug dependency, alcoholism, or eating disorders should seek professional help immediately. When treatment is underway, attending a support group that discusses these problems can also be helpful. There is no need to fight an addiction alone when fellow Christians, counselors, and people with similar problems are willing to share the burden.

I am thirty years old and have a problem with overeating. While obesity doesn't run in our family, I'm about fifty pounds overweight. How can I safely overcome my craving for food?

Several factors usually contribute to gaining weight, which means that losing weight requires more than a simple solution. Bookstores are full of faddish weight-loss books and programs, but seldom do these provide a long-term remedy for overeating and the excess weight that results.

Genetics is one of the key determinants of a person's weight. Your metabolic rate, which has a direct effect on how your body uses the food you eat, is to a great measure something you have inherited. Some people metabolize food more efficiently than others. The conversion of food to energy acts as a stimulus to eat, but it varies from person to person. We have no real control over this process. However, when physical exercise and sensible eating are carelessly put aside, the combination of a slow metabolism, lack of exercise, and poor eating habits spells POUNDS.

Early environment can be an underlying issue of weight problems. Overeating is sometimes related to a pattern of dependency learned from childhood. Those who lack self-assurance often turn to food, drugs, or alcohol later in life, since these substances bring temporary pleasure and relief from the feeling of facing life's problems alone.

Current pressures come to bear as well. A person who is having sexual difficulties may deliberately (or unconsciously) try to look less attractive in order to avoid the possibility of sexual conflicts or rejection.

Some people just like to eat! They don't push away from the food when they ought. Eating has become a pleasant habitual activity, not just a means of refreshing the body's strength. This is not to say we should not enjoy eating, but rather that we need to clarify its relative importance in the whole scheme of life.

While an individual's reasons for overeating are complex and not altogether easy to pin down, the ideas for reversing the problem are fairly simple and straightforward:

Schedule a physical examination. Problems with overweight can be complicated by disease. For example, treating a low-thyroid problem can make a great difference in the way a person feels, and it will help with weight control. Ask your physician for advice on what weight-control regimen is suitable for your age and physical condition.

Start with a well-balanced diet. Fad diets lack an overall approach, which is why their results are so often short-lived. Balanced nutrition is the best diet, which includes eating the proper amounts of the right kind of foods—for a lifetime.

Report to a "monitor" regularly. Accountability keeps you on course. Many diet clinics have their clients "weigh in" once a week, making them accountable to the clinic staff. This helps motivate changes in eating behavior that will lead to permanent weight control.

Do not check your weight more than once a week. Your weight can vary from day to day, depending on intake, fluids, and other factors. Too-frequent weigh-ins can be misleading and discouraging.

Consider possible hidden issues. Are childhood problems or current conflicts causing personal stress? This may involve talking with a friend, a relative, or professional counselor. Try to uncover any unresolved dependency issues—areas of life in which you have not yet established a healthy emotional self-sufficiency. Ask yourself, "Am I depending on food to fill a void in my life?"

Turn to Christ. You should do this with any problem! Become accountable to him for everything about you, including your eating habits.

For a detailed discussion of the Minirth-Meier treatment program for overeating and its root causes and
cures, read *Love Hunger* (Thomas Nelson, 1990).

*Our ninth-grade daughter—the oldest of our six chil-
dren—is very obese. She is a sweet and dependable girl
but began gaining too much weight in the fourth grade.
We have tried everything, including limiting her por-
tions at mealtime and curtailing snacks. Nothing seems
to help. Obesity is not a problem for anyone else in our
family. What can we do for her?*

Many of the weight-loss suggestions in the previous
answer apply to young people, but first you must determine *why* your daughter has been overeating. Start off by
arranging a thorough physical evaluation. Thyroid and
other endocrine disorders can contribute to obesity
because of their effect on metabolism. Although this is
usually not the principal reason for gaining weight, especially in children, it should be explored.

If no medical cause for her obesity is found, it is likely
that something bothering your daughter at home or
school has taught her to establish a pattern of turning to
food for comfort. Consider what pressures might be working on her. Does she have trouble keeping up her grades?
If so, make sure to keep close contact with her teachers
and school advisor to see what help you could give her on
that score. On the other hand, perhaps she is overly shy
and has trouble making friends. There are many subtle
ways by which parents can encourage their children to be
more outgoing (see chapter 5).

Finally, there is the possibility that you have unfairly—
though unwittingly—placed undue pressure on your
daughter at home. In most families, the oldest child (especially if a girl) is expected to help with younger siblings
and household chores—which is just fine *if not overdone.*
Consider whether you may have assigned your daughter
responsibilities beyond what is appropriate for her age. If

that is the case, removing some of that pressure will give her time and opportunity to develop her own special interests. As she begins to take enjoyment in the normal activities of adolescence, she will be less likely to seek solace and pleasure in food.

If you have tactfully explored all the above possibilities with your daughter and still have no clue to the emotional basis for her overeating, gently suggest that a psychological evaluation might be helpful. Unfortunately, parents are the last people in whom some teenagers will confide! Talking to a psychologist and possibly taking some personality tests might uncover why she has become so dependent on food and give her a better perspective for dealing with the problem.

If your physician has not already done so, encourage your daughter to begin a practical weight-loss program that will also teach her sensible *lifetime* eating habits. (Drastic fad diets can be extremely dangerous, especially in the growing years.) Groups such as Weight Watchers and Overeaters Anonymous are quite effective, and many localities have special sessions for young people. Dieting discipline is tough. It ultimately depends on the strength of the dieter's resolve to lose weight—but the accountability that exists in a support group provides an added incentive.

As your daughter makes an effort to control her overeating, it is very important that you affirm her—which does *not* mean nagging or calling too much attention to her progress (or lack of it). She—not anyone else—must be the one to curtail her food intake. Attempts to "shame" her into losing weight will be as counterproductive as trying to hide the snacks at home. She is old enough to find food elsewhere! Above all, be sure your daughter knows that you love her as she is, but that you would like to help. Try your best to enlist the cooperation of the younger children. If that is impractical, at the very least make it unquestionably clear that ridicule of their sister's appearance (or anyone else's) will not be tolerated.

Extreme obesity can be life-threatening. If your daughter cannot overcome her problem in any other way, hospitalization might be advisable. Here her calorie intake would be strictly limited and her health carefully monitored. If such drastic treatment seems warranted, try to locate a Christian behavioral-medicine facility, where the program is centered on scriptural guidelines and the work of the Holy Spirit in the life of the believer.

I am a single mother with a three-month-old son and very concerned about our future. Because I have had no support from my family, late in my pregnancy my problems seemed so overwhelming that I started drinking. When I realized that I was consuming up to a pint of rum a day, I decided to do something about it—fast. This morning I dumped all my supplies of alcohol down the drain, but I am worrying about what effects my drinking has already had on my baby. I know I will be going through withdrawal symptoms. Will he experience them, too? Even more to the point, how can I best control my urge to drink?

There is indeed great concern for a baby whose mother is drinking, especially if she is nursing her child. The presence of "alcohol syndrome" frequently occurs in babies if the mother consumed alcohol during pregnancy, especially if she nurses the child and continues to drink. If your baby is healthy now, perhaps your alcohol consumption has not affected him, which is all the more reason to control your drinking in the future.

Now that you have taken that important first step, take heed of the following suggestions:

1. *See a pediatrician immediately* (if you have not already done so). Explain your situation and have the physician verify that everything is going well with your baby's health. Inquire about possible telltale signs of alcohol withdrawal in your son's behavior and how to handle them.

2. *Take scrupulous care of your own health,* which includes, of course, not drinking. Your baby's welfare depends totally on how well you function as his mother. Single mothers without supportive relatives and/or friends must face most problems alone, so you will need to be especially strong. Tell your personal physician about your problem and ask for advice on how to control your drinking. Tranquilizers may be prescribed to help you through the initial withdrawal period. This is important, since some people have dangerous seizures at this time. If you ever weaken in your resolve not to drink, at least make sure not to have even one drink while also taking tranquilizing medicine.

3. *Find outside support.* You are obviously under great pressure or you would not have started drinking so heavily in such a short period of time. You will need the guidance and encouragement of others. A pastor or other counselor can probably help you deal with your personal stress, but you may also have financial problems that complicate your situation. If that be the case, contact community welfare agencies for help in locating a job and child-care facilities. As for your urge to drink, Alcoholics Anonymous has helped countless others come to terms with why they are drinking and provides an ongoing support system. Most communities have local AA chapters, and some are church-affiliated. Check into this and also consult your local mental-health organization about related resources, many of which are available at no charge or for a fee based on ability to pay.

Is there a relationship between depression and alcoholism?

In some cases there is a definite link, but not always. Each of us reacts differently under pressure. Some develop ulcers or high blood pressure; others abuse alcohol and drugs. Some people become medically depressed because their brain's neurotransmitters do not remain at constant levels (for one reason or another). Research supports the theory that depression and alcoholism have a direct correlation in the history of some families. It is interesting to note that alcoholics may be better able to reject alcohol once treated for depression.

Alcohol is a depressant. It is frequently used as a pick-me-up by people who feel sad and blue because it *temporarily* lifts their mood. But the initial high spirits will fade rapidly and the low mood intensify, making them feel even worse than before they first took the drink.

Alcoholism has a probable genetic predisposition in some people, but is ultimately a choice to keep or treat. Psychiatrists generally believe that early environmental experiences and the repression of feelings probably contribute more to depression than does genetics. And, even if alcoholism is *not* inherited per se, parental example may play a part in setting up a habitual drinking pattern in the children of alcoholics.

Lately it seems that I've been drinking more and more alcohol. I've been told that a drink now and then won't hurt you, and I feel I can control my use of alcohol. Is it really safe to drink at all?

Alcoholism begins with the first drink. No one plans to become an alcoholic. Most heavy drinkers once believed they could control their use of alcohol. In fact, many of them still think they can, even though their aberrant behavior and the empty bottles are evidence that they cannot. "Denial" is a convenient defense mechanism for most alcoholics.

America has over fourteen million alcoholics today, compared with three million in 1950. These figures alone show how widespread this problem is becoming. Valium, sleeping pills, tranquilizers, and other prescription drugs are also widely abused. The effect this has on the individuals and their families is always detrimental and often tragic. In the long run the health of the entire society is at stake.

Beer commercials typically promote alcohol as a part of the "macho" image. But the truth is, alcohol in excess destroys liver and brain cells and can cause an unhealthy increase of enzymes in the bloodstream. All humans have both male and female hormones. In men the liver filters out excess female sex hormones. When men drink they begin to lose that liver function and, as a result, take on feminine characteristics. The "macho" plan actually backfires! These men may eventually become impotent— if they don't succumb to heart disease or cirrhosis of the liver first! Yet, though alcohol does not increase their masculinity, men continue to use it for that purpose.

Magazine ads that portray social drinking as symbolic of "the good life" entrap men and women alike. As the "one or two drinks with friends" or nightcaps before bedtime become habitual, some people find that their drinking is out of control. Then they "need" a drink (or more) to get them through the day or to deaden the pain of coping with a current problem.

One shot of whiskey taken on an empty stomach permanently destroys two thousand brain cells. Regular drinking contributes to lowered intelligence, inability to concentrate, impotence, and depression. Alcohol also lowers levels of serotonin, a chemical important to the brain. Suicidal depression is related to a serotonin deficiency.

With all these facts in mind, make your own decision as to whether or not it is safe for you to have even one drink.

What causes substance abuse, and how can it be treated?

Being overly dependent on external sources of gratification is the main contributing factor to substance abuse. Statistics show that many alcoholics and drug abusers grew up as the youngest in their families and developed dependency needs they could not satisfy in adulthood. In such cases, these last-born were too sheltered. They never learned to make decisions for themselves; their parents thought and decided for them. In adulthood, the overdependence that worked in childhood may be transferred to an addictive substance. The substance abuser's only hope is professional help, which must include counseling on how to become independent from the booze or drugs and dependent on the strength provided by Jesus Christ.

Another inherent cause of substance abuse is the fear of facing painful inner feelings. Addicts often recall not having the freedom to openly express their feelings as children. Later in life they learn to dull their emotional pain by using drugs or alcohol, continuing the habit of denying hurt and disappointment. Therapy is designed to encourage them to tear down the wall of silence and reveal their true feelings to themselves and others. This can eventually lead them to abandon their chemical crutches.

Hospitalization is usually the best starting point for breaking abusive habits with drugs and alcohol. Substance abusers must first escape the stressful environment that is wearing down their emotions. In a caring atmosphere fashioned especially for intensive therapy, many abusers can be helped to get in touch with their feelings and become permanently independent of drugs and alcohol. Hospitalization is a courageous step for those who fear insights into their own buried emotions and motives.

Several aspects of treatment are necessary for long-term recovery from substance abuse:

Medical care is essential. A hospital is the safest place to endure withdrawal reactions. Controlled withdrawal is the most effective means of beating a drug or alcohol addiction. It is also important to the health of the patient that this gradual withdrawal be monitored by a qualified physician. Fifty percent of alcoholics who withdraw and go into DT's (delirium tremens) will die if they are not in a hospital. Many alcoholics erroneously think God will save them physically from the very laws of nature that he created in the first place.

Insight-oriented therapy should supplement medical treatments. Drugs and alcohol are an easy way to deny problems from the past. Substance abuse is a symptom of underlying emotional, spiritual, and/or psychological issues that require the attention of a trained counselor.

A behavioral approach facilitates desired changes. Some people think of alcohol addiction as a disease that is completely inherited, rather than a wrongful but controllable weakness that *may* have some genetic basis. Behavior-modification training must augment medication and counseling if there is to be complete victory over this destructive habit. It should also be part of any drug-recovery program.

Complete change of environment is often needed, especially for addicted young people. It is external pressure that drives some people to drugs or alcohol. When removed temporarily from the stressful circumstances and treated as suggested above, they usually can learn to deal with their problems and conflicts without relying on chemical props.

Spiritual growth is vital to full recovery and ongoing Christian maturity. Personal problems must be faced squarely. This begins with accepting Christ as Lord and Savior and then spending regular quiet time with him to deepen the relationship. Spiritual peace grows through one's trust in God and close friendship with his Son. To the degree that this peace is experienced, an individual finds the strength to deal with his or her inner struggles.

Abusers recover faster and more completely if they have faith in God's ability to see them through their ordeal. "Faith" is sometimes dressed up in fancy descriptions and easy clichés. Yet the simplest axioms are the hardest to live by. Church attendance and Scripture reading feeds faith, giving practical meaning to an abstract ideal. Faith ultimately replaces the illusory and temporary confidence found in drugs or alcohol.

Support groups are important for substance abusers and their families. Alcoholics Anonymous (AA) and Al-Anon are support groups for alcoholics and families of alcoholics, respectively. Al-Ateen is a group specifically for teenagers who have an alcoholic in their families. Even though some of these groups are not expressly Christian, they are often "spiritual" in nature and can be truly helpful. For a Christian, an AA-type group affiliated with a Bible-believing church is probably the best resource. Such a group centers on the person of Jesus Christ as the "higher power" in life, using biblically oriented techniques. Avoid groups that do not have that perspective.

Don't be an "enabler" to substance abusers you know. Never make excuses for them, give them money to continue their habits, or blame yourself for their weakness. Urge these people to seek help, and do not make it easier for them to continue as they are. You may have to watch terrible consequences befall them, but reminding them to seek help is the best thing you can do for them. Because you must not interfere with God's efforts to turn them away from self-destruction, do not allow them to avoid responsibility by becoming overly dependent on you. Love them with a "tough love," even if it means temporarily abandoning them until they straighten out their lives.

My husband is chronically angry and often depressed, sometimes for no apparent reason. He comes from a broken home and his father is an alcoholic. We have been married eight years and have three children. In recent months he has turned physically abusive, and I now fear for my safety. Although he is seeing a psychiatrist at my urging, he still has wild fits of rage, especially when I even hint at leaving him. I love him and want our marriage to work, but I don't know how to handle him anymore. What is your advice?

Your husband should probably be hospitalized until he learns to control these fits of anger. Once a spouse becomes physically abusive, his (or her) family needs to take steps to protect themselves. Although you obviously have compassion for him and seem ready to forgive his outbursts, you must make it very clear that you refuse to tolerate *any* physical expression of his anger. At least for the time being, separation is the wisest course if he refuses hospitalization.

Your husband's childhood experiences have undoubtedly had a marked effect on how he handles frustration today. He has seen conflict lived out between his parents and quite likely harbors bitterness toward his father. He brought his unresolved anger into your marriage and is taking it out on you. Hospitalization will allow him to concentrate on the intensive therapy he needs, and it will almost certainly guarantee your personal safety.

Abusive people usually feel varying degrees of guilt about hurting others and truly want to gain control of their emotions. A small minority, however, have sociopathic personalities that allow them to feel no remorse over their abusiveness. Little hope exists for these antisocial individuals apart from God's miraculous intervention.

An abusive spouse who is basically well-adjusted in other areas, except for periodic lapses into anger, usually responds well to therapy. After one or two months of intensive inpatient treatment, your husband may overcome his grudges from childhood and be able to handle his hostility. If he can learn to recognize the source of his angry feelings and communicate them rationally, he is on the way to cultivating realistic expectations for day-to-day living.

Do not allow him to stay if he is being physically abusive at this time! Simply tell him when he is in a relatively calm mood, "Because I love you, I want you to get help. When your psychiatrist agrees that you are safe to live with, we can be together again. And I will lovingly receive you back." For now, have him temporarily removed from your home since you owe this to yourself and your children. If he will not willingly submit to hospitalization, you may have to seek a protective injunction from the courts and/or relocate temporarily to another environment. (Perhaps there is a "safe house" in your community—consult your local social-services agency.)

You, too, may need counseling to work through your

own anger, hurt, and disappointment. Let your bitterness be washed away by loving forgiveness. Talk to your pastor about this. If you and your husband have not attended joint counseling sessions, you may want to talk to his therapist about the situation, if only to add to the facts he or she already knows. However, because of doctor-patient confidentiality, you will probably not learn very much about what your husband has revealed to his counselor. (You will most likely need a consultation with the therapist if you start procedures to have your husband hospitalized.)

With proper therapy, your husband may learn to handle his angry feelings in nonabusive ways. Then there is considerable hope for your marriage. When he does return home, make it very clear that you will stand for no further abuse.

Two years ago, at the age of fourteen, our son stopped going to church and began to smoke, use drugs, and otherwise rebel. Now he is attending NA [Narcotics Anonymous] meetings, but is down on himself and life, without emotional energy or interest in God. Physicians tell us he is physically healthy. A neurologist who performed a CAT [Computerized Axial Tomography] scan of his brain said there is only minimal brain damage due to the drugs. What can we do to help our son get back on course?

Too many teenagers ignore what they've been told about the dangers of drug abuse. It seems that no matter how much we educate and warn them, they experiment anyway, because of peer pressure or problems at home or school. Some young people have literally burned out their brains on drugs and will spend the rest of their lives without motivation or energy.

If a neurologist has told you the brain damage is minimal, your son's lack of energy and poor concentration are probably related to a depletion of serotonin. Certain drugs, such as LSD and marijuana, lower serotonin levels and cause depression. Anger and guilt can also have this effect. Your son is almost certainly depressed and needs to see a psychiatrist, preferably one with a Christian orientation.

One option is to attend psychiatric outpatient counseling, combined with nonaddictive antidepressant medication to help rebuild his serotonin levels. Having a Christian influence in therapy may help him turn his life over to the Lord. Then your son can begin to grow again—both spiritually and emotionally. He needs a new set of friends who support Christian ideals. This may not happen right away, but a competent counselor can be an effective instrument of God. Ask the therapist whether group counseling with young people your son's age is feasible for him. Many teenagers respond quite positively to this type of approach.

Another option is to place your son temporarily in a Christian behavior-modification medical unit. Teenagers in similar situations profit by spending as long as two months in such a facility, where medication and daily counseling are used to build up their self-worth and confidence. Here your son could learn to be more keenly aware of his feelings and to verbalize them in ways that are biblically correct. Of course, hospitalization is appropriate in severe cases, especially if a young person is in danger of giving up on life by attempting suicide or returning to rebellion and drug dependency.

What is bulimia? How do people overcome it?

Bulimia involves binge eating (usually of food high in starch and sugar content), followed by self-induced vomiting. Laxative or diuretic abuse often accompanies this eating disorder. About one-fifth of female college students and younger teenage girls, as well as a growing number of young men, exhibit some type of bulimic behavior.

Bulimia is caused by many different factors. The influence of society is perhaps the most significant. The current fad that equates "beauty" with a slim physical appearance is taking its health toll, and bulimia is part of the price. Teenagers in particular have a tremendous desire to conform to the "ideal man" or "ideal woman" image. As they enter this confusing period of life, many seek the false security found in having a "perfect body," even at great physical, emotional, and psychological cost.

Ironically, parental influence may also be a key factor. Perfectionistic parents unintentionally pass down their rigid standards to their children, who in turn try to reach these or other unattainable goals. Failing that throughout childhood, young adults continue performing for parental approval. Being attractively slim is one way they hope to win affection or at least attention.

A distorted self-image—a feeling of being "damaged goods"—is commonly seen among bulimics. They don't see themselves as okay, as loved by God or anyone else. This is particularly true of abuse victims. Many bulimics tend to have a mixture of obsessive-compulsive and histrionic personality traits, which include perfectionism, performance orientation, indecisiveness, manipulation, mood swings, and difficulty controlling emotions. On the surface they are excessively devoted to work, longing to be productive to counteract the insecurity that envelops them inwardly. They may crave attention and become perfectionistic performers.

Parents of bulimics typically deny their child has a problem, but most have overemphasized physical appearance and the importance of making a good impression on others. These parents are often overprotective, which hinders the development of a child's autonomy, as evidenced in healthy independence and interest in outside activities.

The symptoms of bulimia and its long-term effects include:

1. Recurring secret binges of high-calorie, easily ingested food
2. Self-induced vomiting and misuse of laxatives
3. Excessive exercise

4. Frequent and dramatic weight fluctuations
5. An awareness that the eating pattern is abnormal, with a fear of not being able to stop voluntarily
6. Depression or moodiness and self-deprecating thoughts
7. Abdominal pain
8. Inability to become physically comfortable (fatigue, weakness, cramps, headaches, heart palpitations)
9. Intense feelings of being cold
10. Heart complications due to electrolyte imbalance
11. Stomach or esophageal ruptures due to binges or vomiting
12. Calcium or vitamin deficiencies
13. Throat irritation
14. Possible precancerous condition of the large intestine

Are you concerned about bulimia? The following traits indicate a tendency to misuse food. The more "yes" answers you have, the more you may be susceptible to developing bulimia or some other eating disorder.

I frequently eat more than intended, especially when bored or lonely.

I understate how much I'm eating or tell myself and everyone else that I intend to start a diet very soon.

I have been eating more food, and more often, in recent months.

At times I spend more money on fast foods than I should.

In the last six months I have started three or more diets (or tried fasting) to prove that I can master my food problem.

I continue to use certain categories of food for comfort even though I know they harm me.

I eat more when under stress.

I feel my overindulgence is caused by problems in my life.

The next characteristics indicate a progression into the more critical stages of bulimia:

My eating continues until late at night and sometimes into early morning.

Cutting back on eating results in headaches, weakness, depression, irritability, or sleep disturbances.

Indulgence in food is destroying or damaging my sense of self-worth.

I find myself anticipating binges and hiding food.

Lately I crave sugary, starchy, or fatty foods.

The amount of money I spend on over-the-counter foods is causing major problems in my budget.

The treatment of *any* eating disorder should be directed toward the entire person—body, mind, emotion, and spirit. There are no quick and easy solutions to this type of problem, and hospitalization is highly advisable. Besides facilitating treatment of the adverse physiological effects that may have already occurred, an inpatient unit allows for intensive psychiatric counseling to uncover the reasons for the inappropriate eating behavior. A Christian-oriented approach will usually reinforce the patient's personal faith system. Behavior therapy can then be used to reinstate healthy eating patterns. Since the underlying causes of bulimia and other eating disorders are often traceable to the home environment, counseling may also be directed toward parents and other family members who might have unknowingly contributed to the patient's distress. During the recovery period, bulimics need their family's understanding, cooperation, encouragement, and—above all—unconditional love.

Cynthia Rowland, a former bulimic who was successfully treated at the Minirth-Meier eating disorder hospital program in Dallas, has written an account of her struggles, *The Monster Within* (Baker, 1984). The book offers much help for bulimics and their families.

Burnout and Workaholism

Burnout—emotional, physical, and/or spiritual exhaustion usually resulting from too much stress—is increasingly a threat to personal well-being and long-term productivity in our society. It especially affects Christians, who may become so committed to a task they believe is God's will for them that they refuse to rest until the job is finished. A problem occurs when their human limitations "finish" them before the goal is reached.

The same type of person falls into the trap of workaholism, which causes personal suffering and emotional deprivation and pain for their families and loved ones. Workaholics bury themselves in work rather than face the other activities necessary for a well-balanced life, particularly those that involve relating with other people.

There are many practical ways to care for one's total well-being by reducing the incidence and effects of burnout. Perhaps you or someone you love is heading toward burnout without realizing it. Or you may be aware

169

of a friend or job associate whose flame of dedication has burned to a flicker. If so, this chapter contains some important information for you.

What is workaholism? People keep telling me that I'm a workaholic. I am a hard worker, but I see that only as a positive characteristic.

Workaholism is an "addiction" to overworking, with a perfectionistic emphasis on performance and a never-satisfied drive for accomplishment.

The presence of workaholism is evidenced by four signs:

1. *A schedule that is too full.* It is not uncommon for a workaholic to work fifteen-hour days, including weekends. Workaholics spend excessive amounts of time on the job, week in and week out. They mistakenly think that the quantity of their work time proves their competence and dedication.

2. *An orientation toward raw performance.* Workaholics talk about specific accomplishments (theirs and those of others), rather than the pleasure of interacting with people.

3. *An inability to say no.* Workaholics take on more work than they can possibly accomplish, all in an effort to please and perform for others.

4. *An inability to relax.* Workaholics cannot seem to enjoy the simple pleasures of being quiet—to relish the beauty of the world around them or savor the joy of personal relationships.

Working hard *is* a commendable characteristic, but falling victim to workaholism is dangerous, both to the worker and his or her family.

It's difficult to admit, but I am a workaholic, especially in my church activities. What can be done to overcome my obsession with busy-ness?

Christians often have more trouble with workaholism than other people, because they convince themselves that the excessive amount of responsibilities they undertake is God's will for them. Fortunately, wanting to obey God makes the solution to workaholism relatively easy. You need an adjustment of priorities more than anything else if you are to rediscover what Scripture teaches is really important—spiritual growth, family values, and—yes— enjoying the abundant life (John 10:10).

Another consideration must be your mental health. Workaholics are of little use to God, their loved ones, or anybody else if they suffer burnout. Although time off for relaxation is a "no-no" to most workaholics, it is essential for balanced living. You need time with your family, time to visit with friends, time for rest and get-away-from-it-all vacations. To turn back burnout, the first step is refusing to become overly committed, even in your church-related activities.

Christian counseling is vital for anyone who is a chronic workaholic. Such counseling will teach you to look at yourself the way God does, as a human being with many facets, instead of the way you have mistakenly learned to see yourself—as a machine or a workhorse. Without the assistance of a wise counselor, relaxing may actually be painful for you; most workaholics feel guilty if they take any leisure time.

One pastor in the Chicago area protects his members from workaholism by not allowing any individual to take on more than one area of service in the church. In most churches, 20 percent of the people do 80 percent of the work, and those 20 percent are usually workaholics. This pastor knows that a person functions best with one ministry and plenty of time for family and spiritual growth.

By rearranging your priorities, learning to relax, and enjoying *all* the gifts God has given you, victory over the nature that drives you will be at hand. This will take time. It also requires a serious study in the art of patience. Gracefully relinquishing to someone else a task you once undertook yourself may also mean recognizing that he or she will not *necessarily* perform to your overly high standards. For more insights into workaholism and its root problems, see *The Workaholic and His Family* (Baker, 1981).

How can I tell if I'm headed toward burnout? My husband and I have two small children. I work nights as a nurse while he takes care of the children. Lately I've begun to feel "wrung out."

The following list of symptoms should help you decide whether burnout is a problem for you. Honestly decide which of these statements applies to you. Put a check next to the ones that do:

___ More and more I can hardly wait for quitting time at work.

___ I feel as if I'm not really accomplishing very much in my job.

___ I feel a lot of pressure and responsibility at work.

___ I'm doing fewer things at work that I like or do well.

___ I often ask myself, "Why bother? What I do on the job doesn't really matter."

___ I don't feel adequately rewarded or noticed for my work.

___ Other people on the job don't pull their share of the load.

___ I'm more irritable at home than I used to be.

___ I wonder if my mate and children appreciate everything I do.

___ I'm not as enthusiastic about our family life anymore.

___ People say I'm too idealistic about my goals for my family.

___ I have begun to have headaches and digestive upsets.

___ My energy level is fading away. I'm tired all the time.

___ I find myself snacking constantly.

___ My general appetite has fallen off.

___ I don't sleep well at all.

___ I have a drink [or take a tranquilizer] to cope with everyday stress.

___ My memory doesn't seem as sharp as it used to be.

___ I find it hard to concentrate or pay attention to a task.

___ It has become a real chore to make decisions.

___ I feel helpless much of the time, as if there is no way out of my problems.

___ Sometimes I think no one really cares what happens to me.

___ I've become quite cynical about people and negative about life.

___ It seems like my life has just about come to a standstill.

If a large number of those statements accurately describe you, professional counseling may be needed for your burnout problem. At the very least, you might consider a change in lifestyle. Burnout affects not only one's attitude in the workplace, but also the tone of family life and physical well-being. (You are probably aware that burnout is an "occupational hazard" for professional caregivers—nurses like yourself, social workers, physicians, and counselors, for example.)

What causes burnout?

Burnout symbolizes the cold ashes remaining where once there was too much fire. There are a number of reasons why a flame of activity flashes out of control and then dies. Certain personality types, such as the obsessive-compulsive (hard-working, perfectionistic), are more likely than others to succumb. Zealous Christians occasionally work too hard, particularly if they want to accomplish much for the Lord, but they, too, are prone to burnout. Elijah was one of the most godly men who ever lived, but at one point he suffered burnout (see 1 Kings 19).

Some people are burned out from the stress of too many life changes or from facing too many seemingly impossible tasks. Others burn out from being too absorbed in their professions. Some lose heart because of anxiety and panic disorders. In extreme cases, burnout victims may even break with reality.

Hidden anger is an underlying factor in most burnout. While this is manifested in all personality types, it is especially true of perfectionists. Having grown up with parents who expected too much, perfectionists learn that nothing is ever good enough. They are so used to hearing the message, "That wasn't bad, but you can do much better," that they become angry with themselves over the slightest imperfections. If their solution—to work ever harder—fails to dissipate the anger, they direct it toward others and further drain their energy reserves.

Another common cause of burnout is guilt, which involves being angry with yourself for doing something that you perceive to be wrong. If something you have done is wrong scripturally, your feelings are *true* guilt. If it is not really wrong, but you believe it is wrong because of parental or other authorities' injunctions, it is *false* guilt. But whether the guilt be true or false, it wears down one's energies and must be dealt with and resolved biblically.

It is not surprising that stress contributes to burnouts. Doing too much on the job, at home, or even in the church can lead to burnout. Women often have complete charge of housework and the children, yet also work outside the home. Having such great responsibilities and an unending stream of chores eventually becomes a consuming flame.

I have a wonderful husband and three fine children. What with all I have to do at home and a job I enjoy, I am finding it hard to keep on track. How can I avoid burnout? My schedule is always extremely full and is about to become even fuller.

Workaholics apparently don't understand Jesus' promise that "My yoke is easy and my burden is light" (Matt. 11:30). In the belief that they are working hard for God, they have convinced themselves that everything they do is necessary. In reality, many potential victims of burnout are driving themselves merely to satisfy parental directives from childhood or to appease their own insecurities. They are either pursuing inappropriate and often unattainable goals or are under the delusion that a high level of busy-ness automatically guarantees that something worthwhile is being accomplished. Such busy-ness may serve as a way to avoid or delay dealing with inner feelings and motives.

To avoid burnout, you must quickly reevaluate what is really important. Without an examination and restructuring of your priorities, burnout is inevitable. An appropriate list of priorities for a Christian should include the following:

Know God better. Develop better habits of *unhurried* devotional study and prayer. Plan for regular quiet times with God in your daily schedule. Perhaps this will work better during the day, instead of trying to get up early and losing sleep to have devotions.

Improve your mental fitness. Get eight hours of sleep each night. Eat sensibly and exercise on a regular basis.

Spend time with your mate. Your spouse should be your top human priority. Schedule time together alone. Have fun! Arrange for the children to sleep over with friends or relatives so you can invest an occasional evening in keeping the love between you flourishing. Too many people put their careers first. This can eventually destroy the significance of the job, but usually not until it has also ruined the marriage.

Spend time with your children. Schedule at least two hours daily and four hours on weekend days for quality time with young children. Older children have their own interests and activities and usually require less personal time with their parents. But be alert to clues that your teenagers need some one-on-one attention. Never schedule weekend business trips more than once a month.

Evaluate your talents and determine how to use them more effectively for the Lord. This doesn't necessarily mean *doing* more. You accomplish the most when serving in the area of ministry best suited to your abilities.

Settle on a career that allows you to fulfill all the above requirements.

Achieving a balanced approach takes time. One week you win; the next you're back juggling priorities. You'll know you're on track when your investment of time begins to pay dividends—the romance in your marriage is enlivened, your children look forward to your company, you feel comfortable and unpressured in church ministry, and your fellowship with God grows closer each day. Don't expect this to happen all at once. In fact, don't ever expect all these things to happen together. Life is not so neat, but balancing priorities is what helps you find your way when it gets "messy."

Learn to be satisfied with accomplishing a few tasks daily. The world will not be changed if you do twice as much. More work will be there tomorrow. Although a Christian always works hard, work is a means, not an end. If you set small, manageable goals for yourself and then strive toward them to the best of your ability, you will reap the recurring sense of achievement that we all need to motivate us onward.

You say your children are "fine" now, but youngsters can burn out, too—especially if too much conflict exists within the family. Children can react to such a situation by becoming hyperactive and may be misdiagnosed as having ADD (attention-deficit disorder), when the real cause is too much anxiety. This is easy to spot because they will show clear signs of irritability and antisocial behavior. Stable, unharried parents who nourish their youngsters with loving attention provide them with the basis for a happy, mentally healthy childhood that will carry through into their adult years.

How can I recover from burnout? Stress and pressure have driven me to the point of suicidal depression. Can you offer some advice to help me overcome the frustration I feel with my problems?

While God is sovereign in our lives, we humans have a free will and must assume much of the responsibility for caring for ourselves. The first step to becoming mentally strong again is to accept responsibility for your life and health. You must have a "take charge" attitude if you hope to outlast burnout. Here are some pointers that should help you:

Take care of yourself—spiritually, emotionally, and physically. This includes exercising at least three times a week, eating a balanced and healthy diet, getting enough rest each night, and tackling unhealthy personality traits. Most of all, it means developing a genuine relationship with Jesus Christ. Reverse any suicidal thinking. If such thoughts are more than fleeting speculations, or if you have attempted suicide in the past, check into a Christian hospital or behavioral medicine unit as soon as possible.

Learn time-management skills:

1. Take inventory of how you use time, marking exactly where your time is spent, wasted, or invested each day.
2. Learn to concentrate on the task at hand, ignoring distractions. Jesus said, "Sufficient unto the day is the evil thereof," which means not wasting today's time worrying about tomorrow.
3. Understand the "big picture" of what you're trying

to accomplish. Plan steps by which you can reach
your long-term goals.
4. Work at being decisive. After gathering the perti-
nent information, don't procrastinate in making
decisions.
5. Learn to delegate. You can't do everything yourself.
Others can do *some* jobs better than you.

Get in touch with your emotions. Laugh several times
each day (Prov. 17:22). Increase the amount of positive
self-talk you do, remembering to say uplifting words to
yourself instead of being critical. Spend more time living
in the present, without focusing on future potential problems or past mistakes. Finally, take time out three times
each week for relaxation and recreation with your family
or for spending time with a friend.
*Practice stress management, using the following guide-
lines:*

1. Learn to say no to excessive demands on your time.
2. Learn when to settle for limited objectives.
3. Learn to respond with less intensity to some of life's
situations. Save your passion for those things you
can really help change, letting God have the burden
for the rest.
4. Learn to limit the amount of major change in your
life.

Spend less time sticking to your habitual routine. Try
to break up your schedule. Diversify and change the way
you do things, particularly the trivialities in life. Don't get
stuck in a rut.
Use your sexuality only as God intended. If single,
remain sexually pure. If married, cultivate sexual intimacy and romantic excitement with your spouse.
Uncontrolled sexuality has a way of distorting the rest of
life's difficulties out of proportion.
Work on your relationships. Do something helpful for

another person at least once a week. Focusing on others teaches us to be less selfish and less preoccupied with our own problems. Beware of envy. Wanting what others have is a tremendous drain on the psyche.

Regularly share your feelings with your spouse or, if you are single, with a close friend or relative. Pent-up emotion leads to frustration, which in turn fans the flames of burnout. Even if married, you might also *occasionally* discuss your concerns with someone other than your mate, someone (same sex as you are) who can be trusted to view your burden from a more detached perspective and will not betray your confidence.

Practice forgiveness and resolve conflicts with others quickly and tactfully. Don't allow hard feelings to develop on either side of the issue.

Nourish your spiritual life. Maintain your communication with God through prayer and by reading, memorizing, and meditating on the Word of God. Apply God's forgiveness to every sin in your life and take steps each day to walk closer to the Lord.

Changed emotions follow changed actions. You will not necessarily feel better right away, but changing your behavior in a positive way will soon be followed by more healthy emotions. God's word is true—we can indeed do all things through Christ who strengthens us (Phil. 4:13).

10

Principles of Christian Counseling

It is very important that anyone seeking guidance for a mental or emotional problem have an understanding of the counselor's "philosophy," since that is what will determine the plan of treatment and ultimately the patient's progress. In any given case, the counselor considers many options. Should medication be used? Group therapy? What is the significance of the patient's childhood to the problem being treated? Would hospitalization be useful? Are all aspects of the individual to be considered important in therapy? The answers to these and dozens of other questions are what comprise a counselor's data bank. While counselors may differ on issues of practice, there are certain key principles critical to long-term effectiveness.

A comprehensive view of the individual is crucial to successful treatment. A Christian counselor recognizes and respects all aspects of each client—mental/emotional, physical, and spiritual. Every human is treated as a complete person in the Lord, not as three separate units: mind, body, and soul. One facet may be considered separately, as long as it is acknowledged to be intricately connected to the other two. In human behavior, the whole is more than a mere sum of the parts.

This section addresses specific questions regarding biblically oriented methods of counseling, techniques of treatment, and how and when a person should be referred for professional advice.

Can't the Bible alone solve a person's problems? It seems to me that if one has faith, counselors and doctors aren't needed to achieve mental health.

Correcting a person's spiritual attitude cannot resolve all his or her emotional problems any more than attending church can heal a broken leg. Focusing on *only* the spiritual or the psychological or the physical basis of a disorder will not produce satisfactory results. Invariably, the factors that affect one part of our total personhood will also affect the others. And, as we have noted in chapter 1, Scripture acknowledges the physical and emotional aspects of man.

Some Christians do suggest that simply reading the Bible, memorizing key verses, and meditating on its wisdom will resolve every psychological problem without professional therapy. Because the Bible presents God's eternal truths and message of salvation, it can heal our mind and emotions to a certain extent. God wants us to use his Word to renew damaged feelings, wash away such spiritually eroding problems as anger, guilt, or bitterness, and generally strengthen our ability to handle the ups and downs of life.

The Bible is fundamental to good psychology, but applying it as a "Band-aid" for *every* physical or mental disorder is more than a simplistic solution—it's dangerous. Equally detrimental to a person's total well-being is expecting medical treatment alone to solve problems that also have a spiritual basis. The Scriptures, medicine, and psychological therapy all have a place in healing the whole person.

Effective treatments arise from a clear understanding of the problem's origin. For instance, an alcoholic has a spiritual problem that can be solved when he comes to Christ. But if the alcoholic develops cirrhosis of the liver from years of heavy drinking, salvation will not heal the liver. Similarly, if a person develops ulcers from a riotous lifestyle, simply applying God's principles will not heal the physical ailment immediately, if at all.

Consider the case of Julie, a committed Christian who functioned well up through her college years. But, after completing school, she suffered from depression and migraine headaches for sixteen years. As she struggled physically, her spiritual life suffered, although she continued her devotions every day, as she had since childhood. Julie was not consciously aware of any sin that could be at the heart of her trouble.

When Julie entered the hospital for intensive therapy, a variety of techniques eventually revealed that she was harboring unconscious bitterness toward her divorced parents. Combining counseling with scriptural insight brought about healing for Julie. She learned to verbalize her hidden anger, especially as she studied the teachings of Romans 12:9–21 on exchanging "vengeance" for love. Finally, she was able to admit her bitterness and forgive those who had wronged her. Her headaches and depressive thoughts are gone.

Faith in the person and teachings of Jesus Christ can work together with psychological techniques to achieve effective healing in many such cases.

An elder in our church recently said that it is impossible for a Christian to be depressed or to need psychiatric counseling for any emotional problem. How would you respond to that?

If people were perfect, they wouldn't need any outside help! But even Elijah and Moses were flawed human beings; both of them needed counseling as they strived to walk with the Lord. Philippians 4:6–8 implies that anxiety is a reality, and that we may need to seek the Lord's help to maintain our inner peace. Because the Bible teaches that prayer is the passageway to spiritual peace, we should ask the Lord outright for his assistance to overcome our every struggle.

However, it is not "un-Christian" to seek counseling for problems we may be experiencing. All of us have occasions when we need the help and advice of our fellow humans (see Rom. 12:3–8). As long as we are seeking God's will and trying to walk with him, it is not inappropriate to talk to a qualified and experienced counselor. The Bible also says that an abundance of counselors is the safest way to make choices. If a counselor can offer genuine insight or solid biblical advice, seek it.

Sometimes a problem that appears to be emotional or spiritual in nature—including depression—requires medical treatment. Just as some diabetics need insulin to stay alive, victims of some types of depression have extremely low levels of neurotransmitters in their brain (serotonin and norepinephrine). Medicine can help this kind of depression. We would hardly deprive a diabetic of medical treatment by saying that "a good Christian doesn't need insulin to overcome diabetes." So why would anyone deprive a severely depressed person of counseling and medical treatment if it could truly help?

Counseling is usually necessary in cases of severe depression. Medication, though needed, cannot resolve the underlying causes of depression, which may include both spiritual weakness and unresolved issues from the past.

How can a person be a "Christian" psychiatrist? Doesn't much of psychological theory ignore or refute what God tells us in the Bible?

Some people who are suspicious of psychiatry fear that it is being placed above God's Word. Most Christian psychiatrists (or psychologists) believe that the Bible must be accorded its rightful position of ultimate authority and that any counseling must find its foundation in that authority. Unfortunately, it is also true that even Bible-believing therapists might inadvertently lead people away from biblical principles. They sometimes encourage assertiveness and "taking charge of your life" to the point where the counselee becomes self-centered and obnoxious. It is easy to see why some Christians shy away from psychotherapy.

Hundreds of psychiatrists are born-again believers, but not all of them are deeply committed to sharing Scripture with their patients. A few are actually ashamed of treating patients in the light of God's Word. True "Christian" psychiatrists have Christ at the center of their counseling practices.

Because God's Word is the basis of *all* truth, psychological theory cannot be considered as one side of an issue and the Bible as the other. Any psychological idea must be tested against God's Word. If it does not match what God says, it must be discarded as untrue; if it does, it can help us better understand the Word—and ourselves. Psychiatric *research* always agrees with Scripture because all truth is God's truth, but psychiatric *theories* are sometimes humanistic and nonbiblical.

Psychiatrists learn certain behavioral techniques that can help people understand and resolve their emotional problems. For example, we sometimes place an empty chair in front of patients who have been molested and ask them to imagine that the molester is sitting there. Telling that "person" how they feel about being molested can facilitate the process of forgiveness, the first step in healing. Patients are often afraid or skeptical of this technique at first, but when they finally do it, their repressed emotions come pouring out. Then, after tears and prayer, forgiveness usually comes.

This Gestalt technique integrates psychology and faith, and it is a powerful tool. The empty-chair *behavior* helps people who have been wronged get in touch with repressed *emotions* that are causing bitterness. It follows *scriptural* guidelines—because God tells us that bitterness is a sin. Once the underlying issues are identified, the individual can deal with them, and the spiritual and emotional problems are healed simultaneously.

We sincerely appreciate the ministers who are winning thousands to Christ, but regret that a few are extremely negative toward psychology. Christian psychologists, too, are trying to win people to Christ. When someone with an emotional problem seeks guidance from a Sunday school teacher or pastor, perhaps that person will be led to the Word of God. However, when the problem is severely disrupting that person's life, we hope that he or she will also be directed toward a Christian psychiatrist who lifts up Christ in the counseling process.

For three years I have had recurring bouts of severe depression and have even considered suicide. Lately I have been seeing a psychiatrist who is not a Christian. He has prescribed medication that has helped a little, but I really don't think my mental attitude is improving. Would I have a better chance of leading a normal life if I consulted a Christian psychiatrist?

If you had an eye disease, you should go to the best opthalmologist in town, whether or not that doctor is a Christian. If you needed surgery, you should consult the best surgeon, even if he or she was an atheist. But psychological health involves the soul and spirit, so you need a counselor whose philosophy is biblically centered.

Seeing this secular-minded psychiatrist for medication has not been a mistake, but medication is not the long-term solution. If a Christian therapist is unavailable to you, ask your pastor to recommend one (unless your pastor has had extensive training in counseling techniques).

If you are depressed to the point of suicide, you definitely need to check into a hospital for intensive therapy and monitoring. It generally takes five or six weeks to overcome serious depression through inpatient care, whereas it might take one or more years to accomplish the same results as an outpatient, even if the psychiatrist has a Christian orientation.

My wife and I were married eight years ago, and we have two children. We're both Christians, and Jesus is the center of my life, but my wife is kind of turned off to the Lord right now. She left yesterday and took the children with her. I'm confused and discouraged but I don't have the finances for expensive counseling. Where can I go for help?

You don't necessarily need money to get helpful Christian counseling. The majority of "counseling" performed in the United States is done by the clergy. Consult your pastor and you will probably find a compassionate person who has a wealth of spiritual insight to offer.

Of course, pastors are limited in complex situations that require considerable experience, training, and/or medical knowledge. For example, they usually don't handle such issues as phobias, eating disorders, or psychoses. Some people hesitate to share personal problems with their pastor because they are afraid their Christian faith will be in question. The truth is, pastors are trained to be shepherds. They want to help their flock in any way they can.

Don't delay visiting your pastor while your heart is tender to God's way. Try to get your wife to go with you. You might say, "Whether you come back to me or decide to leave me permanently, let's at least try counseling."

It is very possible that pastoral guidance will help your wife rediscover her Christian faith, which may be all it takes to bring you back together. Recognize, too, that rarely does *one* partner carry all the "blame" for marital discord. Counseling may well give you insight into your part in the potential breakup of your family.

If your wife refuses to attend counseling, you still need to keep in contact with your pastor. Should your wife eventually choose divorce, realize that you are still a useful person for the Lord. Marital stress is always painful, but your pastor's comfort and advice will be helpful, regardless of whether reconciliation with your wife is possible.

I believe that God has given me the ability to serve as a counselor. However, my career is already established. Since I'm middle-aged, I don't have the time, energy, or money to return to school for a counseling degree. I feel that my many years of experience in life can be used to uplift and encourage others. How can I begin to use my counseling ability to help others?

It has been estimated that pastors do more than half of all the counseling in the United States—and that 25 percent of all its citizens would greatly benefit from such counseling. However, since pastors can spend an average of only twelve hours per week in this work, the counseling needs of a community (or even a congregation) cannot be adequately met by the clergy alone.

Many people, on the other hand, while lacking either professional training in counseling or a seminary degree, have life experiences and spiritual insights that can be shared with others. Sometimes just being a friend and a sympathetic listener can be invaluable to someone who is hurting and needs to share a burden.

Throughout the Old and New Testaments are many passages that illustrate how laypeople have served in counseling and advisory capacities. In fact, the apostle Paul points out this function's importance for church members: "And we *urge* you, brethren, *admonish* the unruly, *encourage* the fainthearted, *help* the weak, *be patient* with all men" (1 Thess. 5:14 NASB, italics added). The italicized verbs in this verse are the very essence of counseling, for they illustrate the balanced approach needed when we seek to guide others.

Here the word *urge* means to exhort others to do what is right in God's eyes. When counselors *admonish*, they are establishing a confrontation designed to persuade an individual to consider the effects of certain wrongful behavior. To *encourage* means to show a sincere interest in the hurts of others and then bolster their efforts at self-improvement. A counselor, of course, can also *help* "the weak" by listening to them and cheering them with positive suggestions and affirmations. Finally, any effective advisor must *be patient* and nonjudgmental of others' shortcomings and failures.

As previously mentioned, we believe it is essential that the Word of God underscore any counseling technique and that scriptural principles be illustrated in the life of the counselor. You must believe in God's power to work in the minds and emotions of all people, since effective Christian counselors respect divine authority and wisdom and know that they cannot be successful through their own abilities alone. This scriptural orientation will automatically add three other necessary elements to a counselor's philosophy: (1) unconditional love for anyone seeking help; (2) a keen perception of the underlying causes of the person's distress; and (3) a recognition of the emotional and spiritual benefits that will result from certain desirable changes in behavior.

The degree to which you keep these principles in mind will determine your effectiveness as a lay counselor. Liberty University (Lynchburg, Virginia) offers some excellent counseling courses by extension. If you are interested in counselor training, you might consider that option.

What is the difference between the conscious, the unconscious, and the subconscious?

Sigmund Freud, considered the "father of psychiatry," theorized that *conscious* mental processes represent what we are thinking and feeling at any given moment in time. *Subconscious* thoughts and emotions are those we can fairly easily call up from our memory bank. On the other hand, the *unconscious* (the "id" in Freud's terminology) includes thoughts, motives, and feelings that are deeply hidden and generally outside our awareness.

Freud was considered a genius for realizing that people have thoughts and feelings they cannot recognize. But the Bible taught this concept centuries before: "Search me, O God, and know my heart. . . . See if there is any offensive way in me, and lead me in the way everlasting" (Ps. 139:23–24). Solomon said, "The lamp of the LORD searches the spirit of a man; it searches out his inmost being" (Prov. 20:27). There are many other passages in the Bible that deal with what we now call the unconscious.

There are many sins, evil thoughts, and ungodly motives hidden in our hearts. In fact, if God showed us everything in our unconscious, we would be overwhelmed by horror. Isaiah came close to experiencing this. When he compared his own depravity to God's holiness and righteousness, Isaiah began trembling and weeping and cried, "Woe to me! I am ruined! For I am a man of unclean lips . . . and my eyes have seen the King, the LORD Almighty" (Isa. 6:5). If we had an X-ray machine for the soul, we could see what needs fixing, but we would be crushed to know all that resides within our deepest thoughts. Jeremiah (17:9) said that our hearts are more deceitful than anything, and desperately wicked, beyond our conscious understanding.

Johann Christian Heinroth was a Christian psychiatrist who lived a hundred years before Freud. About 1800 he spoke of the conscious self, which tells us to do one thing while the unconscious (or "flesh") tells us to do another. He believed that faith in Christ was the only way to deal with this conflict. Heinroth was also the first to coin the word *psychosomatic*, but his theories were rejected because he called for faith in Jesus Christ.

Freud theorized that the *ego*, or conscious self, is a slave to the *id*, or unconscious thoughts and drives. He actually meant that we are prisoners of our depravity and cannot escape its effect. Thus, says Freud, since we cannot win, we should simply give up and try to stay out of trouble without feeling guilty about wrongdoing. The world loves this attitude! Although Heinroth also said that we are motivated by our unconscious, he differed from Freud by claiming that there is a solution—faith in the person of Christ to free us from our evil impulses.

Consider the iceberg analogy. God knows all about the part of you that is under water (unconscious), even though only a little of your true self shows above the surface. As you master your conscious feelings, God allows a little more of "you" to appear. God knows exactly who you are and what you are like above and below the "water line" of your own awareness, but he loves you anyway. It is only when you understand this and place your faith in Christ that you can solve the "mystery" of the three levels of consciousness.

Sanctification (or growth in Christian life) occurs when, under the guidance of the Holy Spirit, a spiritual insight from your unconscious is pushed to your conscious awareness so you can deal with it biblically. When you do so, the Holy Spirit continues to push up these insights so that you continually deal with a new or expanded awareness.

I have heard about subliminal tapes that supposedly heal people subconsciously. What is your opinion of these tapes?

Many distressed people face issues and unresolved conflicts of childhood that need attention. Subliminal tapes cannot achieve this adequately, and personalized counseling is always more effective than tapes for such cases.

Selling subliminal tapes as the ultimate solution to every problem borders on trickery. It may be stretching it, however, to say these tapes cause psychological damage *unless* they substitute entirely for the intensive therapy that may be needed for certain individuals. Personally speaking, however, we do not use them or recommend them.

I am the pastor of a large metropolitan church and have had training in pastoral counseling. After ten years of experience I still have difficulty determining whether a person's problems are primarily spiritual or mental. (I hesitate to refer Christians to a secular psychiatrist, because it may be harmful to their faith.) What guidelines would help me assess whether a given individual is in need of professional psychiatric treatment?

The question of *whom* to refer (and *when*) could be simplified by using five basic criteria. You should refer to a professional therapist anyone who is:

1. *Suicidal* (extremely depressed to the point of hopelessness and despair, whether or not suicide is mentioned).
2. *Dangerous to others* (prone to violence or expressing homicidal thoughts).
3. *Out of touch with reality* (delusional or hallucinating).
4. *Mentally or emotionally out of control* (including certain conditions that may have an organic basis). Here your limited skills and busy schedule will not allow you to handle the situation adequately.
5. *Handicapped by a specific physical or mental disability.* (However, once you have made sure that the individual is receiving proper medical attention, you can be effective as a spiritual advisor.)

This list of categories is not comprehensive, but it serves as a general guideline to what types of problems will need professional attention beyond what you can provide. Of course, the basic question in considering referral is whether the problem is mental or physical, rather than spiritual. For example, under extreme stress, even otherwise well-adjusted Christians may choose not to turn to the Lord for help (or may not know how). As the pressure increases, emotional complications can arise. Is this essentially a spiritual problem? Perhaps so, but certainly both "mind" and "spirit" are involved.

If a pastoral counselee is potentially dangerous to self or others, you should refer that person to a professional without delay. He or she may need immediate hospitalization and/or medication. Such statements as "Life is not worth living," or "Everything seems hopeless," indicate suicidal thoughts and planning, especially if there is a history of one or more suicide attempts. Likewise, you should refer to a professional therapist anyone who is expressing a desire to harm another or who has already established a pattern of physical violence (for example, spousal or child abuse).

It is probably beyond your ability to help a person who has lost contact with reality. This is evidenced by delusions (such as feeling chased by others) or hallucinations (hearing or seeing things that are not present). Since these individuals often misinterpret whatever is said to them, counseling alone is rarely effective. Medication is required to alleviate the faulty mental processes. Only then will the counselee be restored to reality and be receptive to further therapy. If a psychotic person goes six months without medication to correct the dopamine imbalance in the brain, the psychosis nearly always becomes permanent and uncurable. Since 3 percent of Americans (including Christians) become psychotic at some time in their lives, thousands of Christian lives are wasted because their pastoral counselor did not refer them to a Christian psychiatrist who could correct the chemical imbalance with proper doses of select anti-psychotic medications.

A counselee who is extremely euphoric or talkative and very hyperactive may be experiencing the "high" phase of a manic-depressive disorder, in which case a genetic and chemical abnormality is likely present. Dramatic progress can be accomplished with medication. Without it, the patient is dangerous to self, makes extremely poor judgments that can result in financial failure, and is nearly impossible to counsel. Obviously, such a person needs to be referred to a professional.

Another organically based (physiological) problem that requires professional treatment is "hyperkinetic reaction." Many overly active children fall into this category. With appropriate medication, a more acceptable activity level can be restored, preventing the development of secondary emotional problems.

There are probably members of your congregation who have problems directly related to other organically based conditions—a *mental incapacity* due to genetic retardation or organic brain syndrome, for example; a *sensory or neurological disturbance* (as in blindness, deafness, or paralysis); or a *systemic disease* process. Others may have incapacitating neuroses that have physiological symptoms (e.g., extreme insomnia, panic attacks, eating disorders). All these people need special medical attention and the support of appropriate caregivers. But this is no reason to be reluctant about offering your spiritual and emotional counsel, assuming, of course, that their other needs are being addressed elsewhere.

When outside help is deemed necessary, you may refer a counselee to a psychiatrist, a psychologist, or an individual in another field, depending on the specifics of the situation. Again, it is highly advisable that referral be made to a Christian professional who uses biblical principles of counseling. Feel free to request a follow-up phone call from any professional who takes over a case upon your referral. Keep in touch with what is happening to your former counselees, most of whom are probably members of your church family who may soon return as active participants in congregational life. For referral information about the Minirth-Meier Clinic nearest you, call 1-800-545-1819.

11

Theological Issues in Counseling

Religious issues commonly arise in counseling situations, especially since "guilt" (real or imagined) is so often part of any emotional problem. Among the common areas of theological interest are "the unpardonable sin," divorce, sexuality, suffering, suicide, and demon possession. In reality, therapy should be an intensive course in sanctification, during which both the counselee and counselor become more like Christ.

Blending Christianity and psychology is challenging, but it depends on a simple rule: God's Word is absolutely binding. Every psychological theory and technique must be examined in the light of Scripture. Any principle that measures up to that standard is useful; anything that conflicts must be rejected outright or studied further to clarify how it may be corrected.

The questions in this section have a theological emphasis. This is not to say that previous questions lacked religious importance, only that these will be more directly related to the elements of Christian faith.

What is your opinion of fasting? Is it safe medically? Can it affect a person psychologically?

Periodic fasting for spiritual purposes (perhaps once a month) is a medically safe practice for otherwise healthy individuals. No fasting should last beyond twenty-four hours, but a one-day fast gives your digestive system a rest. You should experience no harmful effects. However, prolonged fasting is extremely dangerous and its effects can be fatal, long after the fast itself is ended. (Anorexia nervosa, for example, is an eating disorder that often starts as a so-called fast. The patient uses fasting as an excuse to avoid using food.)

Prolonged fasting can dangerously unbalance the bloodstream's electrolytes, cause hormonal changes, interrupt the menstrual cycle, and create other medical problems. God never intended us to fast to the detriment of our health. And we don't need to fast to prove our spirituality; there are no heavenly "brownie points" for fasting. One estimate says that 15 percent of anorexics die from the effects of too much fasting.

Spiritually-based fasting doesn't have to last for twenty-four hours, since skipping one meal for intensely religious purposes can be as effective as fasting all day. During the time you normally eat, pray or meditate on Scripture. This is a chance to get closer to the Lord and to strengthen your personal relationship with him—and it should be the goal of any fasting.

Some Christians fast mainly so they can brag about it later and tell everybody how "spiritual" they are. If you fast, do all you can to keep it a secret between God and yourself. Keeping a written journal of how fasting is enhancing your relationship with Jesus Christ will make the experience even more meaningful.

What do you believe is the reason for all the physical, mental, and emotional suffering in the world? Is it because we sin?

Sometimes we suffer because we have sinned, but not always. For example, many godly biblical people suffered but had little sin in their lives. Job is an excellent example of this. The sudden loss of a loved one, unexpected financial ruin, and other catastrophes and disappointments can cause tremendous emotional stress for even the most faithful believers. More important than the *cause* of this pain is the *cure*. Although some suffering can be prevented by the way we live, trials and tribulations are a basic part of living in an imperfect world.

All of us know what it means to suffer, but it is important to understand that nothing happens by accident. God has a purpose in all things. Consider the possible reasons for suffering:

To develop certain desirable qualities, such as patience, faith, hope, endurance, maturity, and loving-kindness.

To demonstrate the glory of God. The Bible tells the story of a man who was born blind and later healed by Jesus. The affliction was not a result of sin committed by either the man or his parents, but "happened that the work of God might be displayed in his life" (John 9:3)

To illustrate the power of faith. Scripture's greatest stories are about people who overcame prolonged adversity to accomplish wonderful works for God. In fact, that is the clear message of Hebrews 11.

To learn dependence on God. So often in his writings, when Paul told of his hardships, he called attention to the all-sufficient grace of God. Suffering teaches us to depend on God in times of trouble.

To exalt the sovereignty of God. The reason for some suffering will not be known until eternity. But God's wisdom is supreme. He does as he pleases—and it is forever the right thing to do (Dan. 4:35). God has a perfect purpose for everything that happens to us.

To be able to comfort others. We are to help heal the wounds of others by comforting them as "the Father of compassion" comforts us in our troubles. (See 2 Cor. 1:3–11.)

To keep us humble. We are proud beings, so God occasionally draws attention to our weaknesses reminding us that we are descendants of dust. He does this to make us like his Son, that we may be heirs of grace and the heavenly kingdom. (See 2 Cor. 12:1–10.)

Because of the sinful behavior of others. Others are sometimes responsible for our afflictions. Stephen was a godly man, yet he suffered persecution at the hands of unholy men. Many people are innocent bystanders who suffer pain and grief because of the careless and cruel behavior of others.

Because of man's fallen condition. Part of the curse God placed on humans after the Fall is frailty. When sin took away our immunity to pain and anguish, labor and disappointment entered the routine of human existence. These hardships remind us of our imperfections and our need for God.

For discipline. Trials can be a method used by God to awaken the wayward. (See Heb. 12:5–11.)

Satan seeks to destroy us. We have a powerful enemy who loves to see us suffer. The New Testament warns us to prepare ourselves for "spiritual warfare" with him. (See Eph. 6:10–18; 1 Peter 5:8–9.)

We cause some of our own suffering. When we sin or make foolish choices, we bear the burden of unpleasant consequences. What a great teaching device! But some never learn from their past mistakes.

When suffering comes upon us, we should consider the possible reasons, but then move ahead on our Christian walk. Perhaps changed behavior can ease the pain. God's Word can certainly sustain and strengthen us: "And the God of all grace, who called you to his eternal glory in

Christ, after you have suffered a little while, will himself restore you and make you strong, firm and steadfast" (1 Peter 5:10). God forgives us of sin immediately, but he does not necessarily remove the consequences.

Is the highly emotional commitment of "coming forward" down a church aisle necessary to become a Christian?

You don't have to show anyone but God that you have accepted Christ as your Lord and Savior, but you may choose to do so. When Jesus died on the cross, he paid the price for the sins of all people. He offers eternal forgiveness to those who acknowledge their sinfulness and trust him as Redeemer.

To trust Christ, you must first realize that you need him. God's gift of salvation is free. You cannot earn it; no one can ever be good enough to merit God's love and grace. He saves sinners, not the self-righteous (see Eph. 2:8, 9).

The church invitation can be a wonderful time to signify one's personal devotion to God and his Son. Some churches have trained staff to share Scriptures and elements of the faith with those who come forward. The decisions made at a church altar may be emotional, but they should be based on a long-term commitment. Endurance is one of the hallmarks of genuine faith. "Coming forward" is not necessary for salvation, but in the proper setting, it can be a meaningful experience.

I understand that meditating on Scripture can help alleviate emotional stress. How can I learn to meditate? In particular, must I memorize a verse in order to meditate on it?

While it is not necessary to memorize the verses you have earmarked for meditation, it is helpful to memorize those that are especially meaningful to you. If you have hidden God's Word in your heart, it will be there to help you at times of temptation when you might otherwise have been caught off guard (see Ps. 119:11). Memorizing key verses is one of the best ways to apply Scripture to daily life.

Meditation is different from mere memorization. Here are some suggestions to help you meditate more effectively:

1. Find a quiet place. Occasionally vary the pace by visiting a solitary spot beside a lake or stream.
2. Get comfortable. Relax your whole mind and body.
3. Begin with prayer. Ask the Holy Spirit to guide you into applicable truths as you read God's Word.
4. Read for enjoyment. Go consecutively through the Bible, but don't place any legalistic guidelines on yourself (like so many chapters a day).
5. Stop to think about any passage that stands out in your mind. This is how God introduces us to new truths that can alter our behavior for a lifetime.
6. Consider how what you have read affects you personally. Visualize yourself in the passage. How does it apply to your life and your feelings?

If you would meditate in such a manner for ten to thirty minutes each morning and evening, you could expect to see the following results:

Expanded knowledge and understanding of God's Word

Sharpened insight into how Scripture applies to everyday life

Greater understanding of who God is

Improved physiological benefits (e.g., lower blood pressure)

Prolonged usefulness in the Lord's service on earth

Increased ability to passively resist anxieties

Heightened awareness of inner thoughts, especially your personal blind spots that are hard to face.

These are gains worth striving for—and the daily renewing of mind and spirit *does* take time and effort.

Meditating on God's Word is the key to developing the right spiritual mindset, which is the source of lasting emotional strength and Christian maturity.

Meditation was the subject of Paul's message in Philippians 4:8–9:

Finally, brothers, whatever is true, whatever is noble, whatever is right, whatever is pure, whatever is lovely, whatever is admirable—if anything is excellent or praiseworthy—think [meditate] about such things. Whatever you have learned or received or heard from me, or seen in me—put it into practice. And the God of peace will be with you.

(For further information on the subject of meditation, see Dr. Paul Meier's book *Meditating for Success* [Baker, 1985].)

Are mental illness and demon possession related? Is it possible for a Christian to be possessed by evil spirits?

While the Bible indicates that it is possible for someone to be possessed by demons (e.g., Matt. 9:32; Mark 1:32; Acts 19:13), we have not observed an actual case of this rare occurrence in our psychiatric practice. Through the years, people have been quick to accuse mentally ill people of being demon-possessed. Coincidentally, there has been a recent upsurge of interest in the subject of demons and evil spirits in general. Prominent magazines have had feature articles dealing with Satanism. Films such as *The Exorcist*, have been popular with moviegoers, and best-selling novelists have catered to the public's fascination with the occult.

Increased awareness of evil supernatural forces is a mark of our age, especially among young people. However, much of what is conjectured to be demon possession actually represents psychiatric disorders—hysterical dissociative reaction, obsessive-compulsive neurosis, or schizophrenia, for example.

The current interest in demons has contributed to much

confusion about this issue, not unlike the widespread mis-interpretations that existed in earlier centuries. It is possible for some unstable and impressionable people—chiefly those with hysterical disorders or borderline schizophrenia—to be convinced they are demon-possessed.

Sufferers of "tics" or the jerking body movements and uncontrolled outbursts of speech (often foul) typical of Tourette's syndrome may be mistakenly labeled as demon-possessed. However, in both children and adults, these symptoms can be controlled with small doses of antipsychotic medications, such as Haldol or Clonidine. This is a clear indication that demons are not causing the problem!

Others who are thought to be demon-possessed because they hear voices or have visual hallucinations show improvement after receiving small doses of these medications for only a day or two. The rapid return of normal behavior rules out demon possession in such cases, unless one assumes that demons are afraid of antipsychotic medication!

A Christian's protection from evil spirits is not found in being overly concerned about them, but in having an active awareness of Christ as Lord. The pursuit of God through prayer and studying his Word and continuing fellowship with godly people are the surest ways to prevent demonic influence from becoming a problem. The apostle had that in mind when he wrote: "Put on the full armor of God so that you can take your stand against the devil's schemes" (Eph. 6:11). There are demons and a literal devil because the Bible says so. But the Bible also tells us that the devil will flee from us if we resist him.

How can the Bible's teaching help me overcome my depressive thoughts and other destructive emotions?

Daily adherence to biblical guidelines improves our sense of self-worth and generally bolsters our mental and spiritual health. Usually those who have emotional problems will struggle spiritually, too. "Sanctification" (become more like Christ) includes recognizing emotional conflicts as signals from God that we need to monitor our behavior. For example, anger warns us to slow down, examine the situation, and take the necessary steps to dissipate our hostility constructively.

Holding in anger and bitterness against others solves nothing. The bitterness churns away, tearing up an individual's emotions and often doing much physical damage. Prolonged bitterness leads to chronic, clinical depression. Yet, if the bitter person had applied the basic principles of forgiveness as taught in Ephesians 4:26–32, the anger would have been put away long before it became bitterness. It's a pay-me-now-or-pay-me-later kind of proposition, because forgiveness is frequently the key to overcoming depression. Unless forgiveness is eventually applied, the emotional despair will remain.

In other instances, meditating on verses of encouragement can make us take a positive look at our problems and even help us find solutions. And Scripture reminds us that this life is only the beginning, not the end. If life on earth was all we had to look forward to, who wouldn't be anxious or depressed? But in God's eternal kingdom the believer will be able to say, "Can you believe how uptight we were over the silliest of things!"

I have trouble trusting people, and even trusting God. I believe in Christ as my Savior, but I often doubt my salvation. How can I have peace about eternity?

Faith's foundation must be God's Word. Consider the bedrock of your beliefs. The roots of trust must have fertile soil. If you grow them in the rocky ground of speculation and distrust, your faith is bound to wilt under pressure. Take your Bible and prepare to study some passages that emphasize trust in the infinite protection of our all-wise and all-powerful heavenly Father.

For example, 2 Kings 6:15–17 beautifully illustrates

how God covers the believer with invincible protection. God miraculously cared for Elisha and will do no less for you. We are similarly told in 2 Chronicles 16:9 that God is eager to assist "those whose hearts are fully committed to him." Because Job patiently trusted God, he eventually found great peace and satisfaction (Job 13:15; 42:7–17). Psalm 118:6–7 further assures us that the Lord is on our side and will intervene on our behalf.

Even though people fail us at times, we can always seek refuge in God. We are comforted by his constant presence, as Psalm 139:7–12 explains. We are reminded of God's enduring love in Psalm 136 and his redemptive power in Psalm 129. For these passages of Scripture to have their full effect, you must be confident that God will not reject you. Trust requires vulnerability. If you open your heart to God's call, you can build your trust in him.

Concentrate on following fiercely after God. Become one-on-one friends with him. He wants to reveal himself to you, but he wants you first to trust him. God does not shroud himself in mystery. Instead, he pulls aside the veil, inviting you into the inner sanctum of fellowship with him. You can refocus your perspective on life by seeking—and receiving—eternal insight into the significance of your problems.

See yourself as a member of God's team. With God as your Captain, you can accomplish anything he calls you to do (Ps. 27:1; Phil. 4:13). God is omnipotent and has all the power you need (Jer. 32:27). But you must believe he is willing to unleash it for your benefit (1 Peter 1:3–5). Rejoice in the fact that God never quits, and his mercies never come to an end (Lam. 3:22). What better proof is there than "God so loved the world that he gave his one and only Son, that whoever believes in him shall not perish but have everlasting life" (John 3:16)!

We often see God through "sunglasses" tainted by the color of our earthly father. Being conditionally accepted by an earthly father makes it more difficult to understand

God's unconditional love and grace bestowed on all who depend on Christ for salvation (Eph. 2:8, 9). As you meditate on Scripture passages dealing with the nature of the heavenly father, forgive your earthly father and stop confusing the two.

Afterword

Over the years on our live radio broadcast, "The Minirth-Meier Clinic," we have been asked thousands of questions by our listening friends. The questions most often asked appear in this book.

We sincerely hope and pray that these discussions will help you experience more of the abundant life in Christ. We trust that this book will also enable you to reach out lovingly to believers and nonbelievers alike who have spiritual, emotional, and physical needs. Our goal in life, after all, is not *self-realization* like the humanists. Our goal is the joy of a meaningful life of *self-expenditure* for the service of Jesus Christ and the benefit of our fellow human beings.

Index